FIRST CLASS TEACHING

FIRST CLASS TEACHING

10 Lessons You *Don't* Learn in College

Michelle Emerson

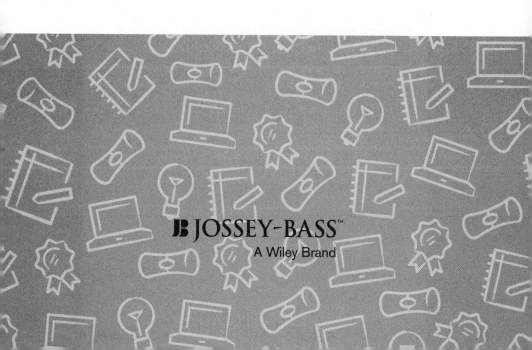

JB JOSSEY-BASS™

A Wiley Brand

Library of Congress Cataloging-in-Publication Data is Available:
ISBN 9781119984900 (Paperback)
ISBN 9781119984924 (ePDF)
ISBN 9781119984917 (epub)

Cover Design: Paul McCarthy
Cover Art: ©Gettyimages/Ediebloom
©Gettyimages/Nycshooter

SKY10044609_031623

To my husband and best friend, Billy, who has been by my side since my student teaching and willingly helped me cut lamination more times than I could count. You set the standard high for teacher-partners everywhere.

To all my students, who taught me far more than I could ever teach them. I am proud to have been your teacher, and don't forget to thank me in all your acceptance speeches. I'm serious.

CONTENTS

ACKNOWLEDGMENTS

I wouldn't have been able to write this book and you wouldn't have been able to read it without the influence and guidance of teachers. Thank you to all the teachers, in their many forms, who make the world a better place through their selfless service.

A very special thank you to my husband, Billy, who has been by my side every step of the way throughout my journey as a teacher. I knew you were a keeper when you voluntarily glued white paper triangles and googly eyes on party hats to create shark hats for my students after only a few weeks of dating, and your support has never wavered. When I first pitched the idea of writing a book, you immediately brainstormed titles and patiently waited for me to bring it to life years later. In the words of *The Office*'s Michael Scott, "Sometimes I'll start a sentence and I don't even know where it's going. I just hope I find it along the way." Thank you for always helping me finishing my sentences. I couldn't have done this without you and I love you more than you know.

To my parents, who have always supported my passions and encouraged my ambitions. I know you really want grandkids, but this book will have to do as my "baby" for now. It might be hard to find a magnet strong enough to hold it up on the fridge but I'm sure you'll figure it out. Thank you for everything you did to get me to where I am today, from giving me that easel all those years ago so I could play school on the front porch to helping me set up my first classroom. I love you both!

To all the individuals who granted permission for their stories to be included in this book. You know who you are, and I am incredibly thankful for our experiences together. You played a role in getting me to where I am today and I can't begin to express how appreciative I am.

To my best friend, Bridget, who always encourages my crazy ideas even when she probably shouldn't. It is so on brand for us to write books at the same time and there's no one else I'd want to go through this challenging but rewarding process with. Thank you for listening to all my rambling voice messages and giving me the much needed confidence boosts along the way. I love you, lady!

To Mr. Pelan, the teacher who made me fall in love with school and pursue teaching (you also inspired me to learn how to play guitar but let's just say I'm a way better teacher than I am a musician). Your passion was infectious, and I strive to positively impact others the way you impacted me. Thanks for getting me the reading intervention I needed in second grade, because otherwise this book wouldn't exist. Seriously, I was on the reading struggle bus and you worked some teacher magic!

To Dr. Gorrow, who made us write down a lifetime goal on the first day of her Classroom Management course in undergrad. My goal was to write a book. Thank you for sharing your experience as an author with the class and helping me believe my goal was actually achievable.

Last but not least, thank you to all the people I don't know personally who have supported me virtually over the years. As an introvert, the thought of sharing so much of my life with strangers on the internet was initially terrifying but stepping out of my comfort zone in that way has allowed me to form so many genuine connections that have improved my life in incredible ways and never would have been possible otherwise. I still don't understand "why me" but I am humbled by your support on a daily basis and will be forever grateful for the opportunities you've brought my way, including writing this book. I hope I can thank you in person someday if our paths ever cross.

YOU'RE HIRED

"How's it going in here?"

I was standing on a chair in the middle of my classroom trying to hang tissue paper lanterns using a paperclip to wedge the string between the light fixture and ceiling tile when I heard a voice coming from my doorway. It's worth mentioning that I'm only five foot, three inches on a good day, so I had the added obstacle of standing on my tippy toes and still barely reached the ceiling. I delicately turned around and braced myself to be scolded by whoever this was at my door because I was almost certainly committing either an OSHA violation, fire code violation, or both.

I caught a glimpse of her face and instantly knew she looked familiar but couldn't remember who she was or where I had seen her before. Did she work in the front office? Was she the librarian? The past two weeks since I was hired as a first-year teacher had been an absolute whirlwind, and I was still trying to catch my breath. I had attended more meetings than I could count and left each one more confused than when I went in. I had met and shook hands with dozens of my new coworkers, only to forget their names seconds later. She smiled at me but waited patiently for my answer before saying anything else.

"Honestly, I don't know what I'm doing and feel like I'm going to throw up but other than that . . . I'm great!"

Humor. This was, and still is, my coping mechanism when I feel uncomfortable.

"Well, let us know if you need anything from us!"

My joke obviously didn't land. In that moment of failed comedy, I realized who she was. I had just told my assistant principal, who had hired me two weeks ago, that I had no idea what I was doing. Crap. I could feel the blood rushing to my face as she disappeared from my doorway, surely headed back to her office to call HR and tell them she had made a huge mistake when she hired me.

"Ms. Ferré?"

Well, that was fast. I was standing directly under the intercom speaker and could practically feel the sound waves vibrating throughout my entire body. This was it. This would be my last moment as a teacher.

"Yes?"

"We're making an adjustment to your class list. We are moving a student to another second grade class just to balance things out. Check your email for the updated roster."

Click. The intercom cut off, and I could finally process everything that had just transpired in the past 30 seconds. Let's see . . . I told my assistant principal I wanted to throw up. Not my best moment but not my worst. I still had a class list, which meant I still had a job. Wonderful! A wave of relief washed over me but was quickly replaced with an even stronger feeling of humiliation. I knew what "balance things out" was code for. I was new, but I wasn't stupid.

I was hired at twenty years old as a first-year teacher with no real classroom experience besides my student teaching internship, which was glorified hand-holding. Word had gotten out to parents in the community that I was inexperienced, and they were requesting to move their children out of my class. Ouch. Don't get me wrong . . . I expected to receive pushback as a new teacher. I anticipated the questions, the concerns, and the doubt from parents because I was feeling the exact same skepticism toward myself. Unfortunately, that didn't make it sting any less. I had exactly one week to pick my pride up off the floor, somehow discover my nonexistent confidence, and step into the spotlight in my classroom.

SHOWTIME

"Good morning! I'm Ms. Ferré and I'm going to be your second grade teacher this year. I'm so excited you're in my class!" I had rehearsed these opening lines in my head about a hundred times as if I was preparing to give an acceptance speech for an award. Spoiler alert: my first day of teaching was *definitely* not an Oscar-worthy performance. Despite my best effort, the words escaped my mouth jumbled and nervy as I greeted students on the first day of school. It worked in my favor, or so I thought, that most of the students were every bit as nervous as I was so they funneled in and took their seats quietly while I aimlessly bounced around the room like a pinball that desperately needed some bumpers for guidance.

"I don't feel so good . . ." A small boy was walking toward me with both of his arms wrapped tightly around his stomach. I recognized his picture from the class list and remembered he was the boy who just transferred from another school within the county.

"You're probably just feeling nervous because it's the first day of school. Here, let me show you your desk and help you unpa—"

My fake-it-until-you-make-it teaching mentality may not have been in the running for any Oscar nominations but

I truly believe this singular moment should have won an Academy Award for Best Live Action Short Film. I was fifteen minutes into my first day of teaching, my shoes were now covered in vomit (more on that in a later chapter), and no less than ten different emotions had swept across my face in a matter of seconds. It was truly an incredible performance. I took an imaginary bow in my head while my audience of wide-eyed second graders eagerly awaited the next scene.

I prayed for some movie magic as I looked at the clock and desperately hoped it read 3:45 so I could go home. Nope. Nine o'clock. The day wasn't a wrap, but it was time to take my students to art, and I welcomed the opportunity to collect myself. I could handle this. I guided my students into something that resembled a line and we chaotically entered the hallway. The line leader followed my directions through the maze of classrooms until we arrived at what I thought was the art room . . . but why were the lights off? My students waited patiently against the wall while I double-checked the placard outside the door. Art. It said art. I peeked my head through the doorway and quickly scanned the room. A feeling of pure panic washed over me as I realized there were no paint palettes or brushes, and, more importantly, there was no art teacher. I reluctantly returned to my former line that now resembled a squiggle of students and decided to improvise.

"We're a little early so we are just going to practice walking in the hallway for a bit." I had bought myself time, but sadly my next move was still a mystery. My eyes darted around as I nervously began leading my class along the colored tile floor without a destination in sight. After what felt like an eternity of aimless walking, I finally made eye contact with another staff member who, thankfully, must have either seen the look of terror plastered all over my face or been able to smell my fear because she stopped to help me without drawing too much attention. We exchanged a few whispers, and she informed me that the art room had been moved to a portable classroom in the fenced area outside of the main school building. In other words, the exact last place I would have looked for it. She deserved a standing ovation for her performance as Best Supporting Role in the horror film that was my first day of teaching.

BEHIND THE SCENES

Like a fish out of water, suddenly I was a teacher fresh out of college and I was terrified to admit I felt more out of place than I ever could have imagined. When I was studying all the educational theories and best teaching practices while earning my degree, everything made sense. I had attended all the lectures, created detailed lesson plans, gotten hundreds of hours of hands-on experience in real classrooms, worked with incredible mentor teachers, and answered questions well enough in my interview to be hired for my current role. In theory, I was ready to be a teacher.

But the moment I stepped foot into my own classroom, I struggled to put what I had learned into practice. It was like giving a student basic directions that were confidently acknowledged as understood with a thumbs up only to have the student immediately forget everything you just told her when she returned to her seat to actually start the assignment (except I was the confused student in this situation instead of the teacher). The issue wasn't the knowledge or understanding, it was the execution. Most of the strategies you learn in college are designed for "ideal" circumstances, but real-life classrooms are far from text-book. This leaves you feeling inadequate, defective, and defeated when you try to implement them but no matter how hard you try, they aren't working. You feel as if *you* are the reason the strategies are failing, when in actuality the strategies are vague, outdated, and not easily applicable to a variety of situations. But regardless of the reasoning, the realities aren't matching your expectations and your passion is fizzling.

I have wanted to be a teacher since I was in second grade myself. It's cliché, but it's true. I held school for all the neighborhood kids on my front porch on the weekends and during the summer, complete with a whiteboard easel I begged my parents for, printed worksheets I somehow discovered for free online, and, yes, assigned homework I fully expected to be completed by the next day. Everyone who knew me knew I wanted to be a teacher, which of course meant they shared their opinions with me, often unsolicited. I heard all the cautionary tales about how hard it would be, how little I would make, and the thick skin I would need to grow if I truly wanted to make my dream a reality. I developed a list of go-to responses I would unconsciously recite any time I faced these warnings. My favorites were, "I'm in it for the outcome, not the income!" and "Teaching is a calling, not a profession," which I often quoted with a smile wrapped so far around my face the corners of my mouth practically met behind my head. I invited every horror story I heard about teaching as a challenge because I thought my work ethic and passion for the profession were unmatched. I sincerely believed I would be an anomaly and thrive as a first-year teacher, but as you can already tell, that wasn't the case.

SETTING EXPECTATIONS

One of the first things you hear echoed in your preparation to become a teacher is setting expectations for your students, so I want to do the same for this book. If you're looking for a manual on how to be the perfect teacher in every situation, I'm sorry to say this book isn't that (and if you ever find that book, please send it my way because I'd love to know how it's done). I don't have all the answers for you, as much as I wish I did. In fact, I'm convinced anyone who tries to persuade you that they have all the answers is lying because we are all just trying to figure out this thing called "life," which came with no instruction manual. I can't give you a blueprint for how to navigate from the first day of school until the last day of school without any road bumps. I can't give you the secret recipe for eliminating every behavior problem in your classroom at any given time. I can't give you a formula to make sure every lesson you plan flows seamlessly when you actually teach it to your students.

Before we get any further into this, I want to make it extremely clear that I am not an expert. Not even close. I taught second grade and fourth grade for seven years before transitioning to a role supporting teachers, so I don't have the most experience, the deepest knowledge, or the biggest résumé in the field of education, and I'm not going to pretend I do. But what I can offer you is my unique perspective. Over the course of my teaching career, I documented a majority of my journey online and shared my experiences with the world, almost like a virtual diary. I was able to capture the highs, the lows, and everything in-between, which allowed me to reflect on my practice and grow in ways I never could have otherwise. I've made a lot of mistakes as a teacher, some of which you will read about in this book and some of which I'm still too embarrassed to think about, let alone write about. But through those mistakes, I've learned and that is the most powerful thing we can do as human beings.

In this book, I want to share my imperfect story, my vulnerable experiences, and the hard lessons I learned to help you realize you aren't alone, but also help you avoid making the same mistakes I did. When you enter your own classroom for the first time after college, you feel like your dreams are somehow coming true and simultaneously being crushed at the same time because you aren't as prepared as you hoped you would be. You're excited and eager, but also confused, overwhelmed, and scared. That's where this book comes in. In the following chapters, I'm going to share the ten lessons I never learned in college that played the biggest role in my growth as a teacher and can help you provide first class teaching to not only your first class, but every class that is lucky enough to have you as their teacher. Teaching is incredibly rewarding, but also incredibly challenging so hopefully this book can make it just a little bit easier for you.

CHAPTER 1

Practice What You Teach

Back to School Night is the teacher equivalent of trying to capture the perfect family photo. If you've never experienced the chaos that is family portrait taking, let me explain. First, everyone gets dressed in matching, or at least coordinating, outfits but it is almost guaranteed that at least one of them gets stained, ripped, or wrinkled before the picture gets taken. Then, all the family members get arranged in a Tetris like format that allows every face to be seen . . . as long as no one moves even half an inch in any direction. Finally, you take a few dozen shots in an attempt to have a single picture in which everyone is smiling. Bonus points are awarded if the tripod falls over halfway through or the photographer makes a small child cry, neither of which are very difficult to achieve.

Back to School Night is basically that same experience, but in a classroom. Leading up to the event, several hours are spent cleaning the classroom, displaying student work samples, and shoving messes into closets only to be rediscovered at the end of the school year. The teacher puts on his or her favorite outfit, which gets drenched in sweat before anyone arrives, partially from nerves and partially from frantically running around the classroom in preparation. The grand finale is when families visit the school and the teacher repeats the same spiel about the curriculum and classroom routines while students and their siblings entertain themselves using any means possible. In other words, it's a complete and utter hot mess.

Back to School Night is stressful, overwhelming, and yes, very sweaty. Despite knowing this, you can't help but be optimistic each year that with a little more preparation and effort, the event can run smoothly. After a few years of teaching and many failed attempts, I finally had a system down for Back to School Night. I had a plastic container packed with all the printed signs I displayed around my classroom to guide families around the stations, a digital slideshow with all the answers to the most frequently asked questions I would get from families, and a table where I would set up all the snacks. I quickly learned that snacks make everything more tolerable, including Back to School Night. My team teacher, Lauren, and I would stay after school and spend about two hours hanging student crafts that had been assembled during the first week of school on pieces of yarn strung across the hallway in a crisscross design. Lauren was almost six feet tall so she had no trouble reaching the ceiling and I was a pro at organizing the papers in a colorful pattern to create that "wow" effect as you walked down the hallway. We truly made a great pair.

During my fifth year of teaching, we decided to up our game and add a banner to the hallway because we had a little extra time to spare. Families would start coming into the school in less than an hour but we were already changed into our fancy outfits and had touched up our hair and makeup. Back to School Night always took place after a full day of teaching, and it *showed*, so both these steps were definitely a necessity. Lauren and I were sprawled out on the hallway floor with a large piece of colored butcher paper, markers, scissors, and glue sticks when suddenly the fire alarm began echoing through the hallways. At that very instant, you could hear the teachers who were still at school groaning at the annoyingly piercing sound but showing absolutely no urgency to vacate the building, ourselves included. We automatically assumed the alarm was being tested so we chose to ignore it and continue preparing for our big night. We resumed decorating our banner until we heard the custodians conversing over the walkie talkies about a strange smell.

"Wait, did you hear what they said?"

We could only make out a few words through the blaring alarm but "gas" and "fire department" were definitely included. That's when it dawned on us . . . the fire alarm was sounding for a suspected gas leak in the school, which meant we did need to evacuate. We popped up off the floor, grabbed our heels, which had been tossed aside while working on the banner, and started sprinting to the front entrance of the school barefoot. The fourth grade wing was located in the back corner of the school so we had a lot of ground to cover. Along the way, we were shouting at the top of our lungs to all the teachers in the building to get their attention.

"*This isn't a drill*! You have to get out!"

"There's a gas leak! We're evacuating! *We repeat . . . this is not a drill!*"

Teachers began flooding out of the classrooms carrying their phones, teacher bags, and half-eaten microwaved dinners. By the time we got to the front of the school, we had an entire herd of frantic teachers jogging behind us, out of breath and profusely sweating. It's always been a running joke (pun intended) that teaching was our form of cardio, but, clearly, sprinting through the school hallways on one of the hottest days of the year is *actual* cardio. We got to the parking lot where our principal, assistant principal, and custodians were casually standing and the ringing of the fire alarm was finally muffled enough to have a normal conversation. Lauren and I proudly announced to our administrators that we ran from the fourth grade hall and alerted everyone along the way that we needed to evacuate. We felt like heroes, but our triumphant story was met with a confused look on their faces.

"Wait, why did you come all the way to the front of the school? Why didn't you just go out of the doors in the fourth grade hall?"

Lauren and I looked at each other and immediately broke out into laughter. We teach our students every single year how to handle an evacuation when the fire alarm goes off and yet, when an opportunity presented itself to practice what we preach to our students, we completely failed. Ask any student, and you will hear the same list of steps repeated: leave behind all your belongings, don't run, quietly exit the classroom, and leave the school through the closest set of doors. What did we do when the fire alarm went off? We took items with us, screamed and yelled while running through the hallways, and took the absolute farthest route possible to exit the building. We basically put on a show of exactly what *not* to do when the fire alarm goes off. It was embarrassing, but honestly not surprising.

NEVER STOP BEING A STUDENT

We all have experience being a student. Whether it was in school growing up, while earning a degree, or trying to learn a new hobby or skill, we've all been in "student mode." When "student mode" is activated, you're a sponge absorbing as much information and experience as you can. You accept the fact that you're an amateur and perfection isn't expected or even possible because you're still learning. You embrace trying new things, making mistakes, and, ultimately, growing through the process. But when you graduate college and step into your own classroom for the first time, it feels as though a switch has been flipped. Suddenly "student mode" has been turned off and "teacher mode" has been turned on. When "teacher mode" is activated, you're suddenly thrust from the passenger seat of the classroom to the driver's seat. You gain control, which comes with added responsibilities related to both your performance as the teacher and the performance of the students sitting before you.

All your education and training has supposedly prepared you for this so the transition should be seamless, but the activation of "teacher mode" comes with a lot of self-imposed and societal expectations. As a teacher, you are now a professional and a role model, which means you suddenly feel the pressure to perform at a higher standard. Especially when you have a room full of students looking to you for guidance, you feel like you're expected to have the answer to every question, a solution for every problem, and mistakes have to be avoided at all costs. This pressure, whether it's externally or internally imposed, is very real and very heavy but the expectation to be perfect is incredibly unrealistic.

Teaching is rooted in people and people are complicated. Over the course of your career, you are going to face difficult circumstances that no amount of education or training could ever prepare you for. You will have students who come to you with heartbreaking stories and less than ideal home lives that take an emotional toll. You will be faced with the moral dilemma of teaching curriculums with fidelity that you know are outdated and don't meet the needs of your students. You will have to manage challenging behaviors with care, caution, and strategic choices. Every single day in your classroom, you will make hundreds of split-second decisions. The bad news? You are going to get things wrong along the way. It's unavoidable. But the good news is, these moments of imperfection are the most powerful moments we have as teachers to act as positive role models for our students.

A strong role model isn't perfect. A strong role model leads others by continuously showing up as the best version of themselves. Role models encourage growth in others by setting an example of humility, self-reflection, willingness to change, and responsibility. Ironically, these are the same qualities we expect from our students. We want them to make mistakes, evaluate their progress, make adjustments, and accept responsibility for their actions. Instead of seeking perfection, we just want students to always show up as their best selves. These expectations are realistic and attainable, which sets students up for success. But when it comes to the expectations we place on ourselves as teachers, we don't hold ourselves to the same standard. We feel embarrassed when we make mistakes and try to mask them from others, refuse to ask questions in moments of uncertainty to avoid appearing ignorant, and evade help from others in fear of judgment and scrutiny of our abilities. The same way our students look up to us for guidance, we need to look to them for inspiration as they continuously model the qualities necessary to grow and improve as individuals. To be a great teacher, you have to practice what you preach . . . or in this case, teach.

REVAMP YOUR EXPECTATIONS

Close your eyes and visualize your idea of the perfect student. How do they act in class? What is their mindset toward learning? How do they collaborate with others? Think about their attitude, behavior, actions, and effort and consider how these elements positively impact their experience as a learner. You might be thinking of a student who walks into your classroom every day with a smile and all the necessary materials (maybe including a coffee for you, but let's not get too greedy), which shows a positive attitude and an eagerness to learn. Every time you ask a question, this student's hand immediately shoots up in the air because he or she is engaged in the lesson and wants to participate. The student you're picturing might be flexible with trying new things, takes risks, and is willing to make mistakes. When you offer feedback, he or she reflects and adapts in order to make improvements and avoid repeating the same mistakes in the future. This student works well with others, enjoys collaborating to gain new perspectives, and values what others have to offer.

This sounds dreamy, doesn't it? Let's come back to reality for a second. Obviously, students seldom possess ALL of these incredible qualities. Some students are always engaged in the lesson but struggle to accept feedback or redirection, while other students are willing to take risks and make mistakes but every group collaboration results in arguments. Just like every other human being, students are imperfect and have flaws, which is to be expected because we've already established that perfection isn't the goal. But as you reflect on the ideal qualities you look for in your students, it is important to be honest with yourself about how many of the qualities you personally possess and consistently practice as a teacher. If roles were reversed, would you be satisfied with your attitude, behavior, actions, and effort?

My first year of teaching coincided with training for my fourth marathon. Don't worry, I already know how crazy I was. While I was constantly exhausted both physically and mentally from all the hours I was working as a teacher paired with all the miles I was running in training, this combination presented me with ample time to think and reflect on my practice. I started every run listening to a murder mystery podcast (I mean, what else would you listen to while running through the woods by yourself?) but my racing thoughts always forced me to pause halfway through. I would think about everything from seating arrangements to lesson modifications and never failed to come up with my best ideas during my long runs.

The more I reflected on the struggles I was experiencing as a first-year teacher, the more I realized my actions weren't in alignment with the teacher I wanted to be. I was beyond frustrated that some of my students never appeared engaged in my lessons yet I scrolled on my phone and chatted with my coworkers during the last staff meeting. I found it disappointing when a student was confused on an assignment and chose not to ask questions for clarification but I stayed quiet during collaborative planning meetings when I didn't understand a component of the curriculum. I felt defeated when I couldn't get my students to cooperate while completing group work yet I never reached out to my team teachers to collaborate on a lesson because I preferred to work alone. In summary, I was a hypocrite. I realized if I was going to expect these characteristics from my students, I had to hold myself accountable and continue practicing these same qualities in my new role as teacher.

Practicing what you teach means placing the same expectations on yourself that you place on your students.

Be Humble

If you expect your students to be honest and admit when they make mistakes, you have to assume the same humility. This includes apologizing to your students if you lose your temper on a particularly stressful day or make an error while teaching a lesson, apologizing to families if you forget to return a phone call or accidentally assign the wrong pages for homework, and apologizing to coworkers if you respond harshly to an email request or don't follow through with your obligations. These moments can be awkward, embarrassing, and sometimes downright cringey but your willingness to admit fault and accept responsibility for your actions allows you to learn from your mistakes so you are less likely to repeat the same error in the future.

Stay Curious

If you expect your students to ask questions and seek help when they don't know something, you have to adopt a similar growth mindset. One of the most pivotal moments of teaching is the first time a student asks you a question that you don't know the answer to. It never fails that it's something simple you feel like you *should* know the answer to, but tragically don't. As soon as the student finishes asking the question, you can feel the blood rushing to your cheeks and you have merely seconds to decide if you are going to make something up (not recommended) or openly admit in front of your entire class that you don't know the answer. It's humbling, but acknowledging that even teachers don't know everything is a powerful opportunity to model for students how to seek new information and get help as part of the learning process.

Work Together

If you expect your students to respectfully work and collaborate with others in the classroom, you have to seek ways to embrace teamwork in the profession. Just to be clear, collaborating with your team teachers does not mean sitting down with your planning books and iced coffees for thirty minutes while mapping out which standards and lessons you are going to teach in the next week or coming month. Creating a basic plan together and ultimately closing your classroom door to teach the lesson your way is simply cooperating, or coordinating at best. True collaboration requires mutual trust, respect, and commitment. You have to establish a shared goal and equally work toward achieving it while connecting different perspectives, opinions, and workflows. It's honestly not surprising some students have difficulty working with others in the classroom considering we still struggle with the process as adults. But, true collaboration is one of the most effective tools we have as educators to meet the diverse needs of our students and overcome the numerous difficulties we face in the profession. So, in the words of Vanilla Ice, "stop, collaborate and listen."

Don't be fooled. Accepting you're still learning and will make mistakes doesn't make all the challenges that come with teaching miraculously disappear, or even make them easier per se. There will be days, weeks, and sometimes even years where teaching feels like a game you can't seem to win no matter how hard you try. These times will challenge you professionally, mentally, emotionally, and sometimes even physically (when you have to rearrange your classroom desks to create a new seating arrangement on a weekly basis, you're *definitely* challenged physically). Thankfully, the nature of teaching comes with a "do over" button every single day.

REPEAT THE LEVEL

Schooling can often feel like you're a player inside one big video game, complete with multiple levels (each slightly more difficult than the one before) and challenging bosses to defeat before advancing from one level to the next. The game opens with the most basic level: elementary school. After mastering the fundamental skills of literacy and mathematics with some social and emotional development mixed in, you are able to move on to the subsequent levels: middle school and high school. You complete the required classes and pass the mandatory exams to earn your diploma and advance to the next level of schooling: college. The level requirements are slightly more difficult but you're able to lean on the skills you've developed in previous levels to persevere and ultimately earn your desired degree. You've obtained the required number of credits, completed your student teaching experience, and passed your certification exams, which means the college boss has been conquered and you're able to progress to your first teaching job. "Teacher mode" has been activated and this is the part of the game where it feels like you're not only advancing to the next level, but have somehow been transported to an entirely different world.

As a first-year teacher, every single day is brand new. You're continuously presented with unique situations you have no experience handling and you have no choice but to figure it out as you go. Intimidating is an understatement.

What most people don't tell you is that when "teacher mode" gets turned on, "student mode" is never actually turned off. Instead, these two modes function simultaneously and you must assume both roles to be successful. As you move into the role of a teacher, you're taking on new duties and developing advanced skills in addition to the responsibilities you maintain as a lifelong student. You have to continue to be vulnerable, ask questions, make mistakes, and learn along the way but now you also have to guide others through the same process. Remember, the next level is designed to be more difficult than the one before. That's part of the game.

The secret to winning is understanding that sometimes you have to repeat a level multiple times before the game-play makes sense and becomes routine enough that you can pass it with a high score. Don't worry . . . you get to repeat the teaching level every single day you walk into your classroom so there's plenty of opportunities for practice and improvement. Despite how it feels, you aren't expected to know all the secret paths or best modes of attack when you play the level the first time. Every other teacher has been in your shoes and knows how it feels to be lost, confused, and overwhelmed during your first year. How did they advance to feeling confident and secure in their abilities to teach? They repeated the same level over and over until they had it figured out.

When our students don't understand a concept, we reteach it. We scaffold instruction, introduce multiple examples, and present the information in new ways. We keep trying until it makes sense.

There will be aspects of teaching that come naturally to you, such as student engagement, providing feedback, or managing data. But there will be other aspects of teaching that take years for you to master. Be patient and keep replaying the level until it clicks. As long as you keep "student mode" activated, you will never run out of lives and can continue repeating the level as many times as it takes to successfully complete it.

GIVE YOURSELF TOUGH LOVE

Tough love is a fairly common practice in the classroom. We might take off points from an assignment turned in late to teach the student a lesson about responsibility or discipline a typically well-behaved student who has an off day or tests the boundaries to communicate consistent expectations. These moments of tough love are never fun or enjoyable for either party involved but they are beneficial in the long run.

Sometimes, we can be our toughest critics. We beat ourselves up over small mistakes and spend more time focusing on the steps we take backward instead of celebrating the steps we take forward. But as our desire to be a great teacher strengthens, our eagerness to accept responsibility for our actions and how they might negatively impact our practice weakens. Our extreme passion clouds our better judgment and we begin making excuses for our flaws and defending our imperfections because that's easier than making improvements. We justify our actions as a way of avoiding uncomfortable growth. We tell ourselves we tried it before and it didn't work, we don't currently have time to try it again, and maybe we will work on it in future but that moment strategically never comes.

As with any area of life, our weaknesses will remain weaknesses if they are never strengthened. You will never become a master at differentiating instruction if you always convince yourself it isn't necessary when you lesson plan. You will never fascinate your students with a captivating science lesson if you refuse to step out of your comfort zone with hands-on lab experiments. You will never cultivate student independence if you always step in and take control because it's easier than taking the time to scaffold the experience for students. There will always be excuses if you seek to find them.

This is where tough love becomes your best friend. When you find yourself falling back into what is easy or avoiding growth because it is challenging and uncomfortable, you have to call yourself out. You have to become the mean teacher who takes points off late assignments and gives detention because you know it is for your own good. Be honest with yourself, recognize when you're justifying flawed actions, and trade your excuses for improvements. Just like with any new skill, it takes time and practice to properly execute tough love. But when carried out correctly, it can be your secret weapon to consistent improvement as a teacher.

YOUR HOMEWORK

Brainstorm a list of values that are important to you. It doesn't have to be fancy. In fact, some of the best brainstorming sessions are the super sloppy ones. Just grab a piece of paper and pencil or open a digital note on your phone and start jotting down words or phrases that come to mind. Here are a few you can reference to jumpstart the process:

- Honesty
- Compassion
- Responsibility
- Growth
- Justice
- Dependability
- Respect
- Service
- Passion
- Efficiency

After you have generated a hefty list, circle or star the three to five values that are the most meaningful for you. Keep in mind, you can always complete this process on your own or you can choose to involve your students because the end goal is to maintain consistent expectations within your personal life and classroom.

Create a list of expectations that represent the values. Consider each of the three to five most important values you selected and how that value could be represented through actions. The expectations should be broad enough to be applied easily to different areas of your life as well as the lives of your students. As you create your list, make sure each expectation contains at least one verb since the expectations are fulfilled through action. Here are a couple of examples for inspiration:

Value: Dependability

Expectation: Follow through on commitments and promises

Value: Respect

Expectation: Listen to and value different perspectives

You can assign a single expectation to each value, multiple expectations to each value, or a combination of both. After you have generated your list, select the five to ten most applicable and significant expectations you and your students can realistically meet.

Post the expectations in your classroom. Now that you have your expectations, it's time to make them visible as a constant reminder.

1. List the expectations: use student-friendly language such as, "In this classroom, we ask questions." and consider adding pictures to represent each one for added clarity.

2. Create a poster: let your students design it, get it professionally printed at an office supply store, or create it digitally and print it poster-size.

3. Choose a location to display it: on the front of your classroom door, above your board, or mini versions on the corner of each desk (yours included).

Give yourself an expectation report card. It's tough love time. Reflect and honestly evaluate how your current actions align with the expectations you have chosen to adopt and give yourself a grade for each one. You can use the standard letter grades or any other grading system you like, but be sure to channel your best "tough grader" mentality. Don't worry . . . your parents won't be checking this report card and you can still reward yourself with ice cream even if you don't get all passing grades.

At minimum, you need to complete this independently so you can review your grades and determine the two or three areas you need to target to improve. But, you can always involve your students in this process and allow them to grade their current performance (and keep their expectation report cards private, of course).

Gather quotes that resonate with you. If quotes aren't your jam, you can use your "no homework" pass to skip this one. Quotes can be cheesy and cliché but they can also make us feel less alone, create memorable ideas, reinforce important concepts, and inspire us to evolve.

Find quotes that echo the expectations you are working toward and post them somewhere you will be able to reference them often. You can compile a list in a notebook or your lesson planner, save them in a digital note in your phone, set them as the wallpaper of your computer, or print them and display them around your desk.

Find an accountability buddy. This could be another staff member at your school, a teacher friend, or even your students (trust me, they *love* to hold us accountable). Communicate your goals and the expectations you're striving to meet with your chosen accountability buddy and share ideas for how they can help you. The conversation might sound something like this:

"I've always struggled with admitting fault so I'm trying to focus on acknowledging and apologizing when I make a mistake. If you notice that I get defensive when I make an error, it would be really helpful if you reminded me that mistakes are a necessary part of growth."

Complete a weekly check-in. I already know what you're thinking.

"My weekly schedule is jam-packed as it is! I don't have time to add anything else!"

I get it. But, progress stalls when we stop paying attention. It's easy to establish these new expectations for ourselves and never follow up on how we are actually executing them week in and week out. Make it a point to check in with yourself as part of your weekly routine, and be as honest as possible. You can use the same grading scale as before and simply note your progress in your planner, a notebook, or with your class. If you need an extra incentive to make it a weekly habit, pair the task with something you enjoy such as eating your favorite snack or follow it up with a fun activity like playing a game together as a class (this is perfect for Friday mornings).

Remember, molding yourself into the teacher you desire to become is a marathon, not a sprint. There will be periods of time when you feel like you're coming in first place and breaking the tape at the finish line and there will be periods of time, often far more frequent periods of time if we are being honest, that feel like you're bringing up the rear and the race crew is picking up the cones marking the course behind you (this actually happened to me in a marathon and I can tell you it is one of the worst feelings). Either way, you have to keep the end goal in mind. Who is the teacher you want to be and what can you do to become that teacher?

The truth is that winners and losers often have the same goals, but the actions they take to try and reach those goals are what differentiate them. "Winning" as a teacher doesn't mean having every day be perfect. It means giving yourself permission to make mistakes, embracing imperfection, and focusing on being 1 percent better tomorrow than you were today. You don't have to do everything to be great at something. Instead, you will see the most growth if you choose one thing to be great at and continue building over time. Regardless of what place you're in, everyone gets to the finish line the same way: one step at a time.

Don't Be a Teacher of All Trades . . . Be a Master of One

I've always prided myself on being a punctual person. I'm not sure if it's the pure satisfaction I feel when I beat the clock or the pure anxiety I try to avoid when I'm not on time, but I have always subscribed to the "if you're not early, you're late" mentality. In elementary school, I was always the first kid at the bus stop, and I have vivid memories of waking up for school an extra hour early, despite not being a morning person, just so I could guarantee I would be ready on time. I learned at a young age I could purposefully set all my clocks five minutes fast, so even if I was running a little late, I would still be on time. Honestly, that little trick has saved me (and my anxiety) numerous times thus far in my life so I would like to take this moment to formally thank my younger self for being so paranoid. It's definitely helped me in the long run.

I'm sure it's no surprise that my punctuality carried over to teaching. While I was almost never the first car in the parking lot because that whole "not a morning person" aspect of my personality only grew as I got older, I did leave home about fifteen minutes before I truly needed to in order to account for any potential traffic on a daily basis and I was always on time to pick up my students from their "specials" (art, music, physical education, and media), which I feel like is the teacher equivalent to being the first kid at the bus stop.

Also, in case you're wondering . . . yes, it was always part of my back-to-school tradition to set the clock in my classroom ahead by five minutes. I typically had to track down a custodian and ask to borrow a ladder to reach the clock, but I made it happen.

Since my excellent time management skills served me so well growing up, I assumed they would do the same for me in my new role as a teacher. I had been able to successfully balance year-round varsity sports with multiple AP classes, a part-time job, and volunteering in high school so there was no reason I couldn't juggle the countless responsibilities that came with teaching. If other teachers could do it all, you better believe I could, too.

After getting hired for my first teaching job, I jumped into preparing full force and spent all summer creating materials for my classroom. Obviously, I was excited for this new chapter in my life but I also had a ton of free time so spending it completing tasks that would save me time at the start of the school year made sense. I was still working my college job as a receptionist (which I would continue to work on weekends and during the summer through my second year of teaching) but my other responsibilities were minimal. I used a foam poster board to create a student job display with pockets to rotate the assigned student each week, turned an organizer designed for nails and screws into a "teacher toolbox" for all the office supplies on my desk, and even hand-painted a wooden stool with my name to sit on while my students were on the carpet.

FYI . . . wooden stools are *highly* uncomfortable to sit on for long periods of time so I suggest adding a cushion or using a chair with back support. You're welcome.

Despite my best efforts to prepare in advance, I felt like I was slowly sinking in quicksand once the school year started. I wanted to deliver meaningful and engaging lessons, so I spent a few hours each week searching online for ideas, creating activities and resources from scratch, brainstorming ways to differentiate, and writing detailed lesson plans. Of course I wanted my classroom to be an inviting and safe space for my students so I spent a few more hours each week cleaning up after school, printing and laminating new posters to display, changing out bulletin boards, and walking around Target looking for adorable but completely unnecessary décor items to buy. On top of that, I still had to take care of my other ongoing teaching responsibilities so I spent the remaining hours in my schedule grading papers, answering emails, communicating with families, and completing paperwork. I somehow managed to squeeze in some time to lock my classroom door and cry when I was feeling particularly overwhelmed, which was basically every day.

Week after week, I didn't feel like I was making any improvement. My lessons weren't meeting all of my students' needs, my classroom was still the first stop on the hot mess express, my assignment turn-in bin overflowed with ungraded papers, my inbox was flooded with unanswered emails, and goodness knows my eyes were perpetually puffy from all the tears I shed. Apparently, I wasn't as great at juggling as I once believed.

I convinced myself I just needed to work harder. I had already been staying after school until five o'clock or six o'clock in the evening nearly every day in an effort to improve in these areas but soon that time extended until eight o'clock, nine o'clock, or ten o'clock at night. On one occasion, the evening custodians knocked on my classroom door at 11:00 p.m. to inform me they were done cleaning so I had to leave for them to lock up the school.

One of my favorite things to do after school was make copies for the upcoming week. It's basically Teacher 101 that the copier is a highly sought after and coveted machine and since most of the other teachers at my school left as soon as the students were dismissed, making copies after school gave me the freedom to queue and print a few hundred pages uninterrupted. Printing a week's worth of copies at one time when other teachers were trying to use the copier was not only frowned upon, but also potentially hazardous when you're a first-year teacher trying to fit in with your school community.

It was a Monday in October and I had decided to have a personal copy party after school to prepare for the week ahead. As soon as my students were all dismissed, I sat down at my desk and queued a class set of copies for several crafts, activities, and practice pages, which translated to around 200 total pages. Our printer system allowed us to send print jobs to the copier in advance but the pages wouldn't actually print until we unlocked the queued job using a code, which was super convenient. In typical teacher fashion, I got distracted straightening student desks, stacking scattered chairs, and picking up broken pencils off the floor so I didn't leave my classroom to retrieve the copies until about thirty minutes later.

Our school had several copy machines located in various rooms around the school including the front office, teacher lounge, and media center for staff members to choose from. Similar to a daily parking spot, most teachers became attached to one copier and only deviated if and when that copier was jammed, which happened frequently but I'm sure that's no surprise.

Sidenote: one of my single *best* pieces of advice for new teachers is to learn how to unjam the copy machine. You can typically find tutorial videos online and most copiers walk you through the places to check for jams on the screen so it really isn't as difficult as it may seem. But most teachers don't want to spend the time it takes unjamming it. You will instantly become honorary Teacher of the Year in your school if you know how to unjam the copier. It's an easy way to make new friends and earn good karma that will come in handy in the future . . . trust me!

My copier of choice was located in the back office of the media center (also known as the library) because my classroom was conveniently located right across the hall. When it finally dawned on me that I had completely forgotten to retrieve my copies, I hurried out of my classroom and burst through the double doors that led to the media center. Again, most teachers in my school had left the building by this time so being quiet was not at the top of my priority list.

One important detail worth adding is that I was wearing slippers. Yes, slippers.

It's no secret that your feet hurt after a long day of teaching. I don't care how comfortable your shoes are, your feet will still hurt. I've tried all the orthotics and padded soles on the market and it still takes several weeks for my feet to get whipped into teaching shape. My solution? I always kept a pair of slippers under my desk to quickly change into after school (and sometimes during my planning time or lunch break if we are being completely honest). I still think this is one of the best decisions I ever made in my teaching career.

Imagine my surprise when I walked into the middle of a staff meeting taking place in the media center that I was arriving half an hour late to . . . in slippers. Mortified doesn't even begin to cover it. I had been so preoccupied with all the tasks on my to-do list that I completely forgot the staff meeting had been rescheduled to this day after school. I would have missed it completely if my little copy party hadn't given me a reason to go into the media center, so at least there was hope I could recover from this lapse of memory. I tried to play it off that I had gotten caught up on the phone with a parent after school as I quickly slipped into the closest chair, but that didn't quite explain my interesting choice in footwear. Plus, I'm sure my flushed face and spontaneous sweating gave it away entirely.

The worst part? I was so thrown off by the impromptu meeting that I forgot to pick up my copies from the printer. Of course, I didn't remember this until I started teaching my lesson the next day and suddenly realized I didn't have any of the papers I needed. Complete teacher fail. It suddenly became clear that the more I tried to take on, the more I felt like I was failing. Something had to change because this obviously wasn't working.

In the grand scheme of things, being late to a meeting or even missing it entirely isn't a huge deal. Over the course of your teaching career, you'll forget to turn in paperwork, show up late to meetings, and get dozens of emails reminding you to complete online training modules that were due weeks ago. It happens and the good news is none of these mishaps are career ending or overly catastrophic, despite how they may feel at the moment. However, they should be a signal to you that you're being pulled in too many directions and need to reevaluate your priorities.

PLUG YOUR BIGGEST LEAK FIRST

Teaching can often feel like you're attempting to bail water out of a sinking ship. During the time you spend checking a task off your to-do list, ten more items are added and, despite your best efforts, you can't move fast enough to successfully accomplish all the responsibilities piled on your plate. You try to prioritize but everything feels important. Lesson planning, student behavior, grading, parent communication, and professional development all seem like vital components of your job that can't simply be ignored without devastating effects. You try to bail the water faster, but this only leaves you feeling exhausted and defeated because your ship is still sinking.

If you're only focused on bailing water out of your ship, your work is never-ending. You feel productive because you're keeping busy, but you don't make any real progress and your ship will continue to fill with water while your frustration grows. But, if you can figure out how to plug the holes where water is entering first, you can stop your ship from sinking.

The holes in your ship are your weaknesses and they're making your job harder than it needs to be. Water will continue seeping in through these holes and filling your ship, which creates more work for you in the future, until you devote time to plugging them. Identifying your weaknesses and working on improving them as soon as possible is the best way to enhance your navigation through rough waters ahead.

Everyone's ship has holes, but not every ship captain figures out how to plug the holes and this is what differentiates the ships that successfully sail and the ships that sink. Even the best teachers have weaknesses, but what makes these teachers great is their ability to recognize and strengthen their weaknesses.

As a new teacher, your ship probably looks like a piece of Swiss cheese. It has more holes than you know what to do with and if you're anything like me, you will try, and most likely fail, to plug them all at once to stop the sinking. But, if you focus on just one hole, you can triumphantly stop the water from flowing in your ship and finally make some progress. Instead of trying to attack all your weaknesses at once, choose a single area at a time to strengthen.

But which hole should you plug first? Focusing on only one area seems like an impossible task when you have so many weaknesses that need strengthening as a new teacher, hence the reason your ship is sinking in the first place. Thankfully, the answer is simple. You plug the biggest hole first. You attack your biggest, and probably most intimidating, weakness.

For most first-year teachers, this weakness tends to be classroom management because it is the area they have the least experience in. As a brand new teacher, you've never had to manage an entire classroom on your own until now and there was no possible way for you to understand all the ins and outs of effective classroom management before you're in the thick of it. But, depending on your specific skill set, your biggest weakness may be found in another area. Here are a few possible areas to consider:

- Pedagogical content knowledge
- Aligning lessons to standards
- Differentiating lessons to meet student needs
- Lesson flow, timing, and delivery

- Student engagement

- Developing and implementing effective assessments

- Collecting and analyzing student data

- Giving detailed and applicable feedback

- Family communication

- Technology integration

- Planning cross-curricular lessons

- Organization

If you're struggling to identify which area is your biggest weakness, look over any previous evaluations you have access to, such as observations during your student teaching or current teaching position and feedback from your mentor teachers, administrators, or coworkers. Keep in mind, you can always request an observation if you don't have any recent evaluations to review and most mentor teachers or administrators are more than willing to offer feedback to help you grow. Take time to read through the comments and consider which area needs the most improvement based on the feedback you received.

When all else fails, ask yourself, "What will have the biggest impact on my students and their learning?" It's easy to lose sight of the bigger picture when you're feeling so inadequate and overwhelmed in the profession, but at the end of the day, teaching is always about the students. Think about which of your weaknesses has a direct influence on your students' learning and target that first.

Remember, after you have successfully plugged your biggest hole, you can move on to plugging the smaller holes that don't sink your ship quite as quickly.

DROP, AUTOMATE, AND DELEGATE

"That sounds good but I just don't have time to add anything else to my plate right now!"

I read your mind, didn't I? The truth is, you're probably right! Our plates are only so big and we can't continue adding to them without also removing items. There has to be a balance of give and take.

Before we consider what might get added to our plate to strengthen our weakness (because yes, you will have to add things to your already busy schedule to make this happen), we need to think about what we can take off our plate. Ideally, you personally would complete all the tasks to get them off your plate but I think it's easy to recognize the unrealistic nature of that expectation. You're only one person and both your time and energy are limited so we have to be strategic.

First, I want you to drop tasks that aren't absolutely necessary or required. Yes, you have my permission to say no to unnecessary requests, refuse to take on extra responsibilities, and simply stop performing the tasks that aren't helping you reach your goals. It's a difficult switch to make, especially if you are a people pleaser like most teachers tend to be, but it becomes increasingly empowering the more you enforce it. Take a look at your to-do list and channel your inner Oprah . . . "You get dropped, you get dropped, and you get dropped!"

Consider stepping back from additional roles you have taken on such as leading committees, volunteering at school events, or coaching after-school teams. As hard as it may be, try to refrain from apologizing for this adjustment because an apology implies that you've done something wrong when in fact, this choice aligns with your goal of improving as a teacher. There is absolutely nothing wrong with trying to be the best version of yourself for your students. If you struggle with confrontation or disappointing people, prepare what you want to say in advance such as, "I'm going to have to step back from (insert role here) because I need to prioritize my time in a way that will help me grow as an educator," or consider sending an email as the initial point of contact. It's less intimidating and it can help you rip off the bandage if you're struggling to say no to your superiors or colleagues.

Dropping tasks doesn't have to mean stopping them entirely. Instead, you can find ways to simply reduce the frequency. If you feel like you are living at the copy machine, you can decrease the number of copies you need for your lessons by teaching students to create their own graphic organizers in notebooks, reusing templates placed inside of dry erase pockets, and digitizing assignments when appropriate. If you spend way too much time changing monthly or seasonal bulletin boards, you can repurpose them as student work displays with clothespins to easily swap out assignments (which a student can do for you).

Next, I want you to automate as many tasks as possible so they seamlessly get accomplished without extra effort on your part. As the term suggests, "automation" refers to setting up tasks to be completed automatically without your intervention. You can use technology as an automation tool to schedule emails in advance to be sent to families or coworkers at a specific date and time, create digital assignments that grade automatically upon student completion, and set your internet browser to open a specific group of tabs all at one time. Outside of the digital world, you can automate tasks in your classroom by assigning students specific jobs such as updating the schedule and date on the board, replenishing supplies, and swapping out manipulatives or books.

Since we're on the topic of giving students jobs, the final thing I want you to do is delegate tasks to others. The saying goes that if you want something done right, you have to do it yourself but I'm here to tell you that in the world of teaching, done is better than perfect. Delegating tasks to students through classroom jobs is a *game changer*! You get items off your plate, students gain responsibility, and you can have someone in charge of finding your coffee when you leave it in random spots around your classroom. It's a win-win-win situation! Your students may not complete the job flawlessly, but sometimes good enough is good enough, especially if it buys you back some time. If you need some ideas for classroom jobs to assign, here are a few ideas:

- Updating the daily schedule and date
- Changing the calendar
- Taking attendance (noting which students are absent so all you have to do is submit it)
- Taking a lunch count
- Delivering papers and materials to other rooms
- Erasing and cleaning the board
- Straightening desks and stacking chairs
- Picking up trash from the floor (yes, there are students who *love* this job)
- Sharpening pencils
- Replenishing supplies
- Returning materials to designated spaces
- Sorting papers turned in alphabetically (this makes it much faster to enter in your gradebook after you grade them)

- Organizing the classroom library

- Assisting the teacher (remember what I said about finding your coffee?)

You can make your classroom jobs as mundane or intricate as you want. You can rotate jobs weekly, have students keep the same jobs all year, or choose something in between. Classroom jobs can be an expected responsibility for your students or you can incorporate real-life finance lessons by paying students for their jobs and allowing them to "spend" their classroom currency on prizes or rewards. You can give the jobs fancy names like "cleanup crew" or "paper patrol" and you can create cute displays that match your classroom theme. There is no right or wrong way to manage student jobs in your classroom so long as the objective of delegating tasks to others is met.

Beyond classroom jobs, delegation can be implemented in instruction to simplify your lesson planning and prep. Instead of creating an anchor chart or poster to display in your classroom while working on a particular unit, have students work in groups to create their own. Students get additional practice during the creation process, which requires higher-order thinking skills, and will be more likely to use it as a reference tool during the unit since they played a role in its creation. This same practice can be extended to the creation of examples, practice problems, and review games and questions by giving students more autonomy and allowing them to submit their own content to be included in lessons. Students enjoy the anticipation and excitement of their submissions getting selected, the content becomes more relevant, which increases student engagement, and your workload as a teacher significantly decreases. Again, it's a win-win-win situation!

Once you can master the art of dropping, automating, and delegating tasks, you will feel your plate becoming lighter by the day. That means room for dessert, right? Well, kind of. It means you have room to work on your targeted area of weakness, which is just as sweet and rewarding!

BE A SPONGE

Have you ever spent so much time around someone that you started picking up some of their mannerisms without even noticing?

My husband is a dancer. Actually, dancer is far too complimentary of a word. Let's try that again. My husband is a shuffler. He blasts music while cooking dinner and shuffles around the kitchen island in the most adorable way possible. On the complete opposite side of the spectrum, my body has rejected dancing my entire life. Fast forward a few months into dating and what do you know . . . I became a shuffler. It wasn't on purpose and I would stop the second he commented, "Was that a little shuffle I saw?" but his habitual dancing rubbed off on me.

I don't know the science behind it, but I've always found that the more time someone spends around someone or something, the more they emulate it. This can have negative results, like when a child starts swearing after hearing curse words at home, but also has the ability to make a positive impact. By surrounding yourself with people who display the qualities you want to build and ideas that mirror the practices you want to implement, it becomes far easier to strengthen your weakness.

The process of professional growth occurs in a cycle. You explore and learn new ideas from others, practice and apply the knowledge in your own teaching, reflect and get feedback, and repeat the cycle as long as needed. This process gets easier when you increase your exposure to learning opportunities and are willing to soak up as many new ideas and concepts as possible. In other words, you have to be a sponge.

If you want to improve your lesson delivery, find ways to surround yourself with people and resources related to public speaking and effective communication. Watch videos of top-rated speeches (they don't have to be related to teaching or education), read articles on effective communication strategies, and observe other teachers in your school who deliver engaging lessons. If you want to improve your abilities as a math teacher, you can read professional development books on how math standards progress across grade levels, watch videos on how to teach various math strategies, and read teaching blogs to find the most effective manipulatives to integrate in your lessons for each topic. If you want to improve your lesson differentiation, connect and collaborate with teachers in the grade levels above and below the one you teach in an effort to better understand the strategies that can be used to support students on a variety of ability levels.

Surround yourself with the people you want to emulate, either physically with the teachers in your school or digitally with other educators you connect with online. Observe them. Talk to them. Ask questions. Get feedback.

Dive deep into the content, research, and professional development space that fits your focus. Read the books. Review the articles. Watch the videos. Stay up to date on the blogs.

Be a sponge and soak in as many new ideas, strategies, and techniques as possible. Implement them in your own practice. Keep what works. Ditch what doesn't. Be patient and you'll eventually start to notice the water in your ship draining.

CELEBRATE TINY IMPROVEMENTS

Hopefully it goes without saying, but the ultimate goal is to plug the holes in your ship permanently to prevent future leaks. Instead of slapping on a piece of Duct Tape and hoping it holds, you need to expand your knowledge, learn new skills, and change related habits to transform your weakness into a strength, which unfortunately doesn't happen overnight. The most sustainable changes in our actions result from slow, incremental shifts rather than rapid, drastic adjustments. These shifts occur with the seemingly miniscule decisions you make on a daily basis. Every interaction you have with a student is an opportunity to demonstrate more cohesive classroom management. Every email you send to families is a chance to convey a connection between school and home. Every assessment you administer allows you to gain valuable information about your students' growth.

As you make these decisions day in and day out, the transformation may appear invisible and nonexistent. You've introduced new classroom rules, established a behavior management system, and are consistently upholding both, but student behavior issues still arise unexpectedly and derail your lessons. When you don't notice any visible progress, you might be left feeling discouraged and even consider abandoning ship.

You can overcome these hurdles by acknowledging and celebrating even the smallest positive changes. If you're trying to strengthen your classroom management and your students get in line without any arguments erupting for the first time all school year, that's a huge win! Cheer for your students! Do a little happy dance! Celebrate the tiny tip-toe you've taken toward your goal because even a small step forward means you're moving in the right direction.

The way in which you celebrate the tiny improvements that occur doesn't have to be fancy. If the improvement involves students, you can allow them to choose a reward to celebrate their success. Your students will most likely be able to brainstorm several ideas if given the chance, but here are a few ways to praise and reward your students or class:

- Perform a class cheer for the student
- Play the student's favorite song (an appropriate version, of course) and have a class dance party
- Allow the student to sit at your desk or use your teacher chair for the day
- Give your class five or ten minutes of free time
- Play a game with your class like charades or silent speed ball (students quickly throw and catch a ball without talking and have to sit out if they drop the ball or talk)
- Allow the class to choose their own seats for the day

If the improvements are personal, you can celebrate yourself in ways that bring you joy such as:

- Listening to your favorite song and having a mini dance party
- Enjoying your favorite snack or meal
- Watching your favorite show or movie
- Giving yourself free time to spend as you please
- Gifting yourself flowers, candy, or a coffee

■ Treating yourself to an item on your wish list

■ Checking an item off your bucket list (maybe save this one for a *big* improvement)

As I mentioned before, it can be difficult to recognize these improvements as they occur if you aren't tracking your progress. Keeping a journal where you jot down your thoughts and feelings as part of a reflection practice at the end of the day can be an easy and effective way to make your progress visible. When you notice your motivation dwindling, you can look back at your entries and see how far you've come. Chances are, you will probably surprise yourself with the growth you've made when you start comparing your progress across several weeks or months rather than day to day.

YOUR HOMEWORK

Do a time audit and reduce distractions. If you're wondering how you're going to fit in the professional development necessary to improve your weakness, it's important for you to understand how you currently spend your time. This is where a time audit comes in. Take a day and write down exactly how you're spending your time in five-minute increments. You can take notes in a physical notebook or just open a note-taking app on your phone, but make sure you honestly document every task you accomplish along with every distraction. Here is a small sample of what that time audit may look like:

6:30 to 6:40 a.m.: wake up and scroll social media

6:40 to 6:50 a.m.: take a shower

6:50 to 6:55 a.m.: get dressed

6:55 to 7:10 a.m.: make coffee and eat breakfast

7:10 to 7:15 a.m.: pack lunch

7:15 to 7:30 a.m.: do hair and makeup while listening to a podcast

7:30 to 7:45 a.m.: commute to school

If you're honest with your time audit, you will be able to identify pockets of time being wasted and distractions to avoid to take some of your time back throughout the day that you can dedicate to your area of improvement. Here are a few examples of ways you can reduce distractions:

- Delete time-sucking apps from your phone (social media, games, etc.)
- Turn on "do not disturb" on your phone
- Place your phone in another room
- Wear headphones and listen to music or sounds that help you focus
- Put a "do not disturb" sign on your classroom door
- Remove clutter from your workspace
- Only open necessary tabs on your computer
- Set timers while you're working
- Determine set times to check your email and texts throughout the day
- Think of a polite response for coworkers or family members who interrupt you such as, "I can help you as soon as I wrap up when I'm currently doing."

Get items off your plate. Chances are, your plate is still pretty full even after you complete your time audit and reduce your distractions. There will also be repetitive tasks that you have to complete on a daily, weekly, and monthly basis and these tasks could easily fill up your schedule if you aren't completing them efficiently. Batch these tasks as frequently as possible. If you are new to batching, think of it as washing an entire load of laundry at once instead of washing each article of clothing individually. It may take a little bit longer initially, but it saves you ample amounts of time in the long run. Here are some tasks you can consider batching:

- Lesson planning (example: plan all your whole group lessons, plan all your small group lessons, create all your teaching slides, and find or create accompanying activities for an entire week at once)

- Making copies (example: queue all of your copies, print them off, cut pages as needed, and organize them for an entire week at once)

- Grading (example: circle all the incorrect answers, write the final grades, write all the comments, and then enter all the grades in the gradebook for several assignments at once)

- Answering emails (example: reply to all your emails once in the morning and once in the afternoon)

- Family communication (example: schedule a month's worth of weekly emails you send to parents with reminders at one time)

Create a list of tasks related to your focus. Once you've determined your biggest weakness, think of actions you can take to strengthen your abilities in that area. You can keep this list in your lesson planner or in a note-taking app on your phone and when you feel like you aren't making progress, you can reference it and determine the next step you can take. Here are some examples of tasks you could add to your list:

- Reading professional development books

- Reviewing new research articles

- Attending workshops and conferences

- Watching related videos

- Listening to related podcasts

- Researching leading professionals who specialize in that area

- Finding ideas and strategies online through social media platforms

Move the dial every day. You have to prioritize strengthening your weakness on a daily basis to develop the practice as a habit and actually make progress toward your goal. Moving the dial simply means performing small actions to continuously move forward instead of remaining stagnant or regressing backward. Take time every single day to work on a task related to strengthening your weakness, which can be selected from the list you created in the previous step. You might choose to block off a thirty-minute time period every day, save a spot on your daily to-do list, or work a task into your morning or evening routine to ensure you are always moving the dial forward.

Follow your productivity body clock. This one goes hand-in-hand with moving the dial every day . . . make sure the time of day you're choosing to devote to your professional growth aligns with your body's natural rhythm. Everyone's internal body clock and workflow habits are a little bit different and you may find that your productivity is at its peak in the morning, afternoon, or evening. The actual time of day is less important than the alignment with your productive rhythm to ensure you're fully focused and attentive. If you plan on reading a book to learn about classroom management strategies just before you go to sleep each night but you have a habit of falling asleep on the couch from pure exhaustion, you need to reevaluate your plan. Choose a time of day when you feel the most motivated, have the most energy, and are the least distracted.

Maximize small pockets of time. If your schedule is far too busy to devote large chunks of time to completing these tasks, incorporate them in the small pockets of time you have throughout your day. Reference your time audit and consider when you have downtime. Here are a few ideas for ways to maximize your downtime to strengthen your area of weakness:

- Listen to a podcast while you get ready or eat your breakfast in the morning.
- Carry a book with you to read while you wait for meetings start.
- Watch a video while preparing dinner or washing dishes.
- Search specific hashtags or catch up on social media accounts that focus on the area you're trying to improve while using the bathroom. (I know, it's gross but let's be honest . . . we all scroll on our phones while on the toilet so we might as well use that time to our advantage!)

Keep in mind that everything in life operates on a system of give and take (more on that in Chapter 10). The time you dedicate to strengthening your biggest area of weakness means giving up the other tasks you would do normally during that time. You might find that these small pockets of time are better spent talking to your coworkers, watching your favorite show, or doing nothing at all because those small moments of peace reduce your stress and bring you joy and that choice is equally valid and commendable. There is no right or wrong way; there is only what is right or wrong for *you*.

Making small improvements doesn't require complete devotion. It only requires effort, consistency, and patience, all of which can be achieved without revolving your entire life around teaching. If you constantly keep your head down and focus on nothing but the skill you're trying to improve, you will miss some of the best aspects of teaching, which involve the people you get to form connections with.

CHAPTER 3

Relationships Aren't Built in a Day

"This is so stupid!"

Those are the first words I remember this student saying (we'll call her Mary). My students were drinking "jitter juice" (a combination of Sprite and Hawaiian Punch) to calm their nerves on the first day of school. In full transparency, I was enjoying a cup as well since it was my first year of teaching and I desperately needed *anything* that would help me feel like less of a nervous wreck. While sipping their drink, students had to create a corresponding recipe for their own "jitter juice" with a list of ingredients that ease their anxiety in new situations, such as their favorite stuffed animal or a hug from a friend. Mary hated the drink, hated the assignment, and hated her new second grade teacher (or so it felt).

I was determined to win Mary over. I made sure to greet her every single morning when she walked through my classroom door. My bright and cheery "Good morning Mary!" was often met with a scowl and maybe a mumble of "hello" if I was lucky. Week after week, I would ask her about her hobbies and favorite TV shows or movies in hopes of gaining any insight into her interests, but "I don't know" and "nothing" were less than helpful replies. I would include her name in practice problems we completed in class, which sometimes elicited a slight smile as she read them. The smile always vanished the second I made eye contact with her but I knew I had seen it. I caught glimpses of her opening up to me and that was all I needed to continue pursuing a connection with her.

After a few more weeks of daily "Good morning Mary!" greetings and inquiring "Did you catch the new episode of *Odd Squad* last night?" (I did finally learn her favorite TV show by the way), we had a breakthrough! Mary wanted to have a "lunch bunch" with me.

My students earned points for completing various responsibilities around the classroom and then could redeem their points for different prizes including candy, school supplies, a stinky feet pass (they got to take their shoes off in the classroom for the day), and a lunch bunch in which they got to eat their lunch in the classroom with me. Mary had always redeemed her points for candy, until now. Now, she wanted to eat lunch with *me*, the teacher I was convinced she hated.

Here's the kicker . . . I wasn't feeling well on this particular day. Besides the general overwhelm and stress, one of the worst parts of your first year of teaching is that you get sick *a lot*. You're exposed to a plethora of new germs in a classroom and it takes time for your body to build immunity. I had woken up with a sore throat, which wasn't severe enough to take a sick day but was intense enough to be annoying and negatively affect my overall mood. As excited as I was that Mary finally requested a lunch bunch with me, I began to worry about her motive. I had shared with my class that I wasn't feeling great, so maybe she wanted to eat lunch with me to somehow make me feel even more miserable. I hate admitting that my mind went there, but our track record was less than stellar.

Every time I felt like I laid another brick in the foundation of our relationship, an earthquake would come out of nowhere and topple our progress. Mary and I would connect and have a great conversation one day, and the next day she would toss the entire contents of her desk on the floor after getting upset with me. I always felt like I was walking on eggshells around her and was worried this lunch bunch would end up being our biggest earthquake on record.

I walked my class to the cafeteria and waited just outside the entrance while Mary purchased her lunch. I was desperate to initiate conversation as soon as we entered the hallway to walk back to my classroom in hopes of starting this lunch bunch off on the right foot. My eyes scanned her tray and noticed she had two wrapped ice cream treats piled next to her hot dog and tater tots. Bingo.

"Wow, you must really like ice cream!"

As soon as the words left my mouth, I could feel an imaginary hand smacking me in the forehead. I should have asked what her favorite ice cream was instead of making a judgmental comment about the volume of her dessert selection. My entire body tightened while I anticipated her reaction.

"Actually, one of them is for you . . . you said your throat was hurting so I thought it might help."

I just stood there in the middle of the hallway with my jaw wide open, feeling utterly shocked but also flattered at the same time. Not only did we avoid a potentially cata-strophic earthquake, but Mary had extended me an olive branch in the form of an ice cream treat. I felt like I was in the middle of a stereotypical TV sitcom when the audience members let out a choral "awww" in response to a sweet moment between characters, except this moment was even sweeter because it was really happening (and because ice cream was involved).

Mary and I made great progress. We still had our ups and downs but we were finally having more ups than downs. That is, until April rolled around. April was filled with noth-ing but downs. Outbursts. Yelling. Crying. Every time I tried to connect with her, she would push me further away. It didn't make sense. We were doing so well! She was finally opening up to me and I felt like she genuinely started to care about me as much as I cared about her. Then I got the phone call.

"Can you have Mary pack up all her things and come down to the office? Her mom is ready to get on the road!"

"Wait, I didn't know she was going on a trip. When is she coming back?" I curiously replied.

"She isn't. This is her last day. Her family is moving and she's going to a new school."

Suddenly it all made sense. Mary knew she was moving but never told me, at least through her words. Her actions clearly communicated that something had changed, but I never considered the reasoning behind the misbehaviors. I was too focused on the way they were making my job as a teacher harder and more frustrating.

I hate to admit this, but I felt a small sense of relief when I got that phone call. The past few weeks of outbursts had been unbearable. I felt like I had done everything I possibly could to try and build a relationship with Mary but it wasn't working. Maybe we just weren't meant to get along. Maybe I just wasn't the right teacher for her.

In the weeks after Mary left, my job did become a lot easier. I had fewer behavior issues to deal with, I wasn't as mentally and emotionally exhausted, and I officially could see the light at the end of the tunnel. I had almost survived my first year of teaching.

During the last week of school, I received another jarring phone call while my students were at lunch.

"Mary and her mom are here in the office and want to see you."

I felt like I was being summoned to the principal's office to be reprimanded for not knowing how to better manage her behavior or failing as a new teacher. As I walked to the front of the school, my mind cycled through all the situations we had encountered together and tried to figure out where I had gone wrong.

As I made the last turn toward the office doors, I was suddenly engulfed in one of the tightest hugs I have ever experienced. Mary ran to me at full speed and wrapped her arms around my torso as if she were holding on for dear life. She had tears streaming down her face, but these weren't "I hate you" tears like I had seen in my classroom. These were "I miss you" tears.

I squeezed her back while her mom explained that her new school was already on summer break so they traveled back to Maryland to visit family. Mary's only request for the trip was seeing me because we had never said goodbye when she left in April. In fact, her last words to me had been "I'm so happy I'm leaving your class!" It was a particularly rough day for us.

That was the last time I ever saw Mary. She didn't say a word to me that day, but she didn't have to. I felt every ounce of respect, trust, and love we had built together in the embrace.

RELATIONSHIPS OVER EVERYTHING

When you're studying to become a teacher, you hear all about the importance of building relationships with your students. Your professors tell you to connect with students on a personal level to make them feel supported and cared for. You've seen all the cliché movies where the teachers bond with struggling students and leave a lasting impact on their lives. You may even have had a personal experience with a teacher growing up that made a difference in your education. Relationship building between teachers and their students appears to be all sunshine and rainbows until you spot the dark rain clouds far in the distance that no one warned you about.

There are a few key challenges that aren't commonly addressed in college or within the teaching community. First, it's preached that relationships need to be the foundation of your teaching practices but no one explains how to actually build them. If you're outgoing and interacting with others comes naturally to you, building relationships as a teacher may be a piece of cake. But if you're anything like me, your reserved and kind of quirky personality makes it far more difficult. Either way, you will most likely encounter students you struggle to connect with and spend hours researching novel ideas only to find vague suggestions such as "talk to them" or "care about them." You feel like the solution should be obvious yet it's nowhere in plain sight.

Second, the feel-good movies lead you to believe that student connections can be formed overnight, like a two-piece puzzle that snaps together without any difficulty. This may be the case for some students, but others take time. A lot of time. For some students, it feels like you're putting together a thousand-piece jigsaw puzzle and nearly half the pieces are missing. You have to keep trying pieces in different places until they finally interlock, you struggle to see the bigger picture scattered among all the intricate details, and you consider abandoning it completely many, many times before you finish. Just like solving a puzzle, you have to be patient and continue devoting time to building the relationship day after day (and sometimes week after week and month after month). This becomes increasingly difficult when it doesn't feel like the progress you're making matches the time and effort you're putting in.

Third, relationships are easy to make a priority at the beginning of the school year when your schedule is more forgiving and the responsibilities haven't piled up quite as high. When you're under pressure to move through the curriculum at a prescribed pace, prepare for looming observations, and just survive from day to day, relationship building is one of the first things to get moved to the back burner. Instead of greeting your students at the door each morning, you find yourself standing behind your desk frantically answering emails that have accumulated in your inbox. You're too swamped trying to plan and prepare tomorrow's lessons to even think about making positive phone calls home to student families and you find your mind drifting to the lengthy to-do list you have formed inside your head instead of listening when your students tell you about their weekend. You formed strong relationships at the start of the school year, but that foundation is quietly crumbling under all the weight you feel on your shoulders as time goes on.

Finally, relationship building doesn't end with your students. It is equally important to build relationships with their families, coworkers, administrators, and other members of your community. These connections are easily overshadowed but hold significant power to strengthen your experience and impact as a teacher. A strong relationship with a student's family can help you navigate behavior or academic challenges, coworkers can offer you support or advice, administrators can facilitate your growth as an educator, and community members can offer unique perspectives and bring new experiences to your classroom. You may not even realize you don't have a strong relationship with one of these stakeholders until that relationship is tested, which presents additional challenges in an already demanding job.

The most meaningful relationships you form as a teacher extend far beyond stereotypical icebreakers in the classroom and cordial hellos in the hallway.

They are time consuming.

They demand hard work.

They require purposeful and ongoing commitment to flourish.

But when done right, the relationships you develop with those around you can transform your life both in and out of the classroom.

TAKE A VOW (AND A STEP)

Building these relationships is definitely not as serious as committing to a marriage, but they can still benefit from a few vows. These vows become the cornerstone of your commitment by providing clear intentions, helping to guide your actions, and giving meaning to the relationship you intend to build. The connections you develop with students, their families, and your coworkers should center around three simple vows, which, ironically, all begin with vowels:

1 Make the individual feel accepted.

2 Make the individual feel important.

3 Make the individual feel understood.

These feelings are at the core of what every human being wants and being able to elicit these feelings through your words and actions is essential to forming a successful relationship. But how do you do that exactly?

Every interaction you have is an opportunity to evoke these feelings. This includes every email you send, every phone call you make, every gesture you use, and every word you speak.

I know, it seems daunting and intimidating to think of these relationships as a series of hundreds or thousands of small steps that eventually lead you to your destination, especially when the destination is nowhere in sight. But rather than overthinking the process of getting from point A, where you don't know someone at all, to point B, where you have connected and developed mutual respect and trust, just focus on the next step.

What is the single next move you can make to strengthen the relationship? What can you say or what you can do to make the person feel accepted, important, and understood? Here are a few ideas to get you started:

■ Learn to say their name correctly (ask them directly or consult someone who knows them personally).

■ Make eye contact when you're having a conversation.

- Invite them to join you in an activity (eating lunch, playing a game, or attending an event).

- Ask them questions and show interest in their answers.

- Make note of their likes, dislikes, and interests.

- Give them your approval by nodding your head.

- Acknowledge the small things they do verbally or in a note.

- Tell them you are proud of them and explain why.

- Offer to help them with a task.

- Send or show them pictures, videos, or items that reminded you of them (use your professional discretion to do this in an appropriate way).

Relationship building is a journey. Sometimes you'll be able to sprint full speed ahead and other times you will find yourself on the sidelines, sweaty and out of breath. You can slow down, take a break, and even stumble along the way but as long as you stay focused on taking one step at a time, you will always know exactly where to go next.

FLIP THE SWITCH

Relationships can be fulfilling and rewarding, but they also can be messy. Disagreements occur. Arguments erupt. Feelings are hurt. In its simplest form, a relationship is just a connection between people, but our human emotions add a thick layer of complication over an otherwise straightforward concept. Our emotions can play tricks on us. They can make us believe we saw or heard things that simply weren't there, and that single moment of misinterpretation can have devastating effects.

If you read a blunt email from a parent and interpret the tone as harsh and condescending, you might convince yourself the parent must not like you and purposefully avoid interacting with them during dismissal. Or maybe you feel disrespected by a student raising his or her voice in class and you assume the student is impolite, which impacts the way you treat them in the future. Sound familiar?

As humans, we all decipher situations differently based on our prior experiences, and a relationship can easily be tainted by assumptions and misunderstandings. To successfully build authentic relationships, you want to avoid these pitfalls by adjusting your mindset before, during, and after points of contact. You have to flip the switch on your emotions and interpret the situation objectively, which is obviously easier said than done.

In emotionally charged moments, start by always assuming the best of intentions. Give the individual the benefit of the doubt, and trust they are doing the best they can at that time. We all know that may not be the case always, but believing it's true will alter your response positively. At the end of the day, you can control only your own actions. Assuming the best of intentions can help you avoid doing or saying something in the heat of the moment that you might later regret once your emotions have subsided.

Let's say that the email you received from a parent was questioning the strategies being taught for a particular math concept. Rather than assuming the parent disagrees with your teaching practices or believes your instruction is inadequate, flip the switch and assume the parent wants to develop a deeper understanding of the strategies being taught so they can be reinforced at home. This shift takes practice, especially if your initial reaction is to assume the worst of intentions, but training your brain to automatically give the benefit of the doubt is powerful.

The next step is to look for the communication behind the words or action, which is sometimes buried pretty deep below the surface. Take a second and ask yourself, "What are they *really* trying to tell me?" The words you hear and the actions you see are often incomplete messages that lack context or manifestations of a deeper need that is more difficult to communicate. Reading between the lines will allow you to complete the message or fulfill the true need.

When a student raises their voice at you or another student in class, consider why the student may be increasing his or her volume. It's possible the student comes from a large family and the only way to be heard at home is by raising their voice. The student may be trying to tell you he or she doesn't feel heard in your class. Rather than interpreting the action as disrespectful or assuming the student is impolite, flip the switch and work together to find more appropriate forms of expression for the classroom.

Again, relationships can be messy. You can assume the best of intentions, look for the communication behind the words or actions, and still encounter bumps along the road of your relationships. In these moments, remind yourself that you are a team and you already know how this ends. As long as this is a relationship you intend on keeping, this rough patch ends with you still being a team . . . you just have to figure out how to get over this bump first. Being a team means you both have the same goals, but your way of achieving those goals may look different. Flip the switch from "I" to "we" and find ways to achieve the shared goal that are beneficial for both of you.

ADD FUEL TO THE FIRE

I have never been camping but I have seen enough episodes of *Survivor* to understand the effort that goes into constructing and maintaining a fire. You have to gather enough dry kindling to capture the initial spark and then continually add fuel in the form of sticks, logs, and other flammable objects to keep the fire burning. Without proper fuel, even the most intense, blazing fire will eventually dwindle and burn itself out.

Relationships are the same way. Beyond the initial efforts, they require ongoing maintenance to continue thriving. Without small gestures of appreciation, periodic check-ins to initiate contact, and open and honest communication, even the strongest relationship will weaken. The most vibrant and illuminating relationships are fueled continually by intentional action.

Once established, the relationships you have formed can be maintained over time through persistent effort, continuous contact, and preserved trust in the form of follow-through and honesty. Below you will find a list of example actions you can utilize to maintain student, family, and co-worker relationships. Most of the suggestions can be molded easily to fit a variety of relationships, while some are geared more toward one specific group, such as students. These actions are all simple to implement and aren't overly time consuming, but can have a big impact on the sustainability of a relationship.

Ways to put forth effort:

■ Give genuine and specific compliments.

■ Leave sticky notes with words of encouragement.

■ Give surprise treats (such as trinkets, snacks, cards, etc.).

■ Offer your help (such as doing a favor).

■ Do things without being asked.

Ways to keep contact:

■ Be the first person to reach out.

■ Send a text or email to check in.

■ Call or send a voice memo to express your gratitude or appreciation.

■ Spark conversation by asking questions.

■ Give your undivided attention.

Ways to preserve trust:

■ Use eye contact, proximity, or a secret signal (such as tugging on your ear or scratching your nose) to communicate discretely if a change of behavior is needed.

■ Follow through with tasks you agreed to do (such as completing a form or implementing a class reward).

■ Be intentional with your words (say what you mean and mean what you say).

■ Apologize if you react poorly or make a mistake.

■ Take action to prevent making the same mistake again.

Once a relationship is well-established and appears to be flourishing, it's easy to go into autopilot and assume the relationship will sustain itself without intervention. You stop reaching out as often. Your thoughtfulness fades. You become distracted during conversations. It happens slowly, sometimes so slowly you don't even notice the subtle changes until the flames of your relationship have dwindled to a mere pile of coals. Just like a fire, the intensity of a relationship may fluctuate over time but the embers can always be reignited so long as they are never allowed to burn out completely.

YOUR HOMEWORK

Do a relationship brain dump. Set a timer for two minutes and try to write down all of your students' names from memory. After the timer ends, cross-reference your brain dump with your class roster to determine which students you forgot to add to your list, or didn't come to mind in the allotted time. These are the students you need to build stronger relationships with. Repeat this process and try to list all of your coworkers including grade-level teachers, paraprofessionals, special-area teachers, support staff, cafeteria workers, custodians, and front-office staff. Depending on the size of your school, you may need to increase the timer (allowing roughly four or five seconds per staff member is reasonable).

If you're great with names and successfully list all of these individuals in the time allotted, an advanced version of this exercise involves listing everything you know about each person on your list. You can list their favorite color, the names of their pets, their hobbies, and everything in between. You'll quickly find that some lists are far more extensive than others, which gives you valuable insight into where your relationships may be falling short.

Choose relationships to build or strengthen. Review your brain dump results and choose one student (or family) relationship and one coworker relationship that either hasn't been built at all or needs strengthening. You can target additional relationships in the future but focusing on one in each area initially is the most realistic and attainable goal.

Audit your beliefs. Think about each individual and consider how your mindset could be negatively affecting the current relationship as it stands. Ask yourself the following questions:

- What words come to mind when you think of this person?
- What do your actions (or lack of actions) communicate to this person?
- What is your body language like around this person?
- What assumptions have you made about this person?
- How might individual differences impact the relationship?

Take time to recognize any biases you may have toward this person and actively work to interrupt them by questioning your assumptions, learning to respect and value any differences you may have, and practicing empathy.

Create an action plan. Brainstorm a list of steps you can take to strengthen each relationship. These steps need to be specific, actionable, and able to be completed within the next two weeks. Here are a few examples for each group:

Students:

- Have a lunch bunch together in your classroom or sit next to them in the cafeteria.
- Create a handshake together (the crazier, the better).
- Incorporate their name into assignments.

■ Plan a lesson around their interests.

■ Play a game of their choice together at recess.

Families:

■ Make a positive phone call home.

■ Share photos or videos of the student in class.

■ Send an email to check in and offer support.

■ Invite them to an upcoming school event.

■ Send home a simple questionnaire to ask for honest input and feedback.

Coworkers:

■ Strike up a conversation during a meeting or in the teacher's lounge.

■ Leave an encouraging note in their mailbox or on their desk.

■ Check in on them (a simple, "Hey, how's your day going?").

■ Offer to do a favor for them.

■ Surprise them with their favorite drink, snack, or candy.

After you have created your list, take a few minutes to schedule these actions into your calendar so you know exactly when you will complete them or add them to your to-do list so you don't forget.

Hold yourself accountable. Commit to performing two or three of these actions a week for each relationship you are trying to build. At the end of each week, check in with yourself to make sure you completed your commitments and decide on the actions you will take the next week. You can write them down on a sticky note you keep on your desk, schedule them on your calendar, or add them to your to-do list. Repeat this process for a month and then reevaluate which relationships in your sphere still need some TLC.

Your experiences as a teacher will seldom match what you see in the cliché movies, especially when it comes to building relationships. There will be some students, families, and coworkers who you struggle to connect with, there will be relationships that dwindle over time, and there will be unforeseen obstacles that arise and complicate the process. But to mirror the theme of almost every feel-good movie out there, the most difficult things are also the ones most worth doing.

The time and effort you put into building relationships with those around you will not only make your job as a teacher easier, but more fulfilling and meaningful. These connections are what keep you going in the toughest moments, which are often spontaneous and unpredictable. During those times, you need a support system that is already established and reliable because plans frequently change but personal connections can last a lifetime.

CHAPTER 4

Pencil It in But Play It by Year

For teachers, field trips are a lot like reality TV shows, pineapple on pizza, or any other polarizing subject— you either love them or hate them. I, myself, love reality television, love pineapple on pizza, and especially love field trips. Whether it's a museum you've visited a dozen times or a smelly dairy farm riddled with dirt and muck that will certainly find its way back into your classroom, experiencing a field trip through the eyes of your students is magical. You get front-row seats to witness their wonder, curiosity, and awe throughout the entire adventure. Sometimes those front-row seats are tattered and located in an ancient yellow school bus with no air conditioning, but it's still worth it.

But there are two main reasons field trips are so polarizing: 1) they are absolutely *exhausting* and 2) they require *a lot* of planning. Number 2 is why I love them so much.

As a Type A teacher, I always looked for a reason to make a list so field trip planning was right up my alley. I had all the forms submitted, buses secured, and permission slips drafted well in advance. I created a detailed checklist to follow in the weeks leading up to the field trip to ensure nothing was forgotten and I always brought a bookbag jam-packed with everything imaginable so if something went wrong, I was prepared. I had a first aid kit to treat any minor injuries. I had a foldable plastic poncho and small umbrella that could be used if it rained. I had trash bags in case any students (or chaperones) got bus sick and I even had mints ready for after. There was nothing a field trip could throw at me that I wasn't ready to handle.

If those sound like famous last words, it's because they were.

It was my second year of teaching and my second graders and I were departing on our biggest, and most exciting, field trip of the year. We were on a standard, yellow school bus heading to an interactive children's museum about two hours away from our school. This was a fairly extensive ride for a class of seven-year-olds on a bus with no bathroom, but if you've ever tried to book a charter bus, you know how expensive they are. A school bus was the only affordable option so we made sure to take several bathroom trips before boarding the bus and stopped halfway for one more, just in case.

Miraculously, we made it to the museum without any accidents and were ready to enjoy the exhibits! Each chaperone group went their separate ways and agreed to meet back at the bus at 1:30 p.m. I had a group of five students who were eager to eat their lunch as soon as we arrived, despite it being only 10:30 in the morning. They convinced me they were starving after the bus ride, which definitely was an exaggeration, but I obliged since eating and discarding the lunches would free up space in my bookbag.

As with most field trips, my students had been instructed to bring their lunch in disposable bags and avoid packing glass containers that could easily break during the trip. We sat down at a table and began unpacking the contents of our lunch when I noticed a student pull out a coffee drink in a glass bottle. It wasn't broken, so that was a relief, and the fact that the student believed their young, energetic body required caffeine in the form of coffee for this field trip did make me laugh.

In a matter of minutes, our table was covered in an assortment of empty Lunchable® containers, torn fruit snack wrappers, and crushed juice boxes. I volunteered to take care of the trash and was determined to make it in one trip, even though the trash can was only a few feet from our table. As I reached to push open the swinging door on the front of the trash can, I heard the glass coffee bottle shatter across the tile floor. Apparently the "no glass" rule was more for the clumsy teacher than it was the students.

Without even thinking, I reached down and started picking up the glass shards with my hands, which of course resulted in a tiny sliver of glass getting lodged in my palm. Thankfully, I meant it when I said I was prepared for everything. I got out a small pair of tweezers from my bookbag and was able to remove the glass from my hand. Crisis averted.

The remaining few hours at the museum went off without a hitch. My students and I climbed through obstacle courses, put together puzzles, participated in hands-on workshops, and explored water exhibits. I'm not sure who enjoyed it more—me or my students. Before I knew it, 1:30 had rolled around and I was standing at the front of the bus taking attendance before we headed home. I checked off the final student, gave the bus driver the go ahead, and let out a sigh of relief as I sat down in my seat, only to discover that something was missing.

My phone.

I patted my pockets and frantically unzipped all the compartments of my bookbag one more time. Nothing. One of the chaperones in the seat directly behind me sensed my panic and agreed to monitor the students on the bus while I went back inside to search for my phone. I was embarrassed, but also incredibly grateful. I sprinted off the bus and began retracing all of my steps in my mind. This museum has over 80,000 square feet of exhibits spread across three floors. Basically, I was screwed.

I quickly decided my best option was to go directly to guest services and check for a lost and found. My face must have had "desperate and frantic teacher" written all over it because the employee behind the counter greeted me with, "What can I help you find?"

"My phone . . . did anybody . . . do you have . . ."

I was out of breath, and my mouth and brain were no longer functioning together. Thankfully the associate was able to put my jumbled words together and handed over my phone. On the walk back to the bus, I convinced myself that the worst of it was over and I could relax on the ride back to school.

Wrong.

About thirty minutes into the two-hour trip, I opened the maps app on my phone to see how far we were from the Chesapeake Bay Bridge, which connects the western shore and eastern shore of Maryland. I knew we should be close but when I zoomed in to locate the little blue dot that displayed our location, it was nowhere near the bridge.

Directions have never been my strong suit, but this definitely didn't seem right.

When you leave Baltimore headed south, there are two main highways you can take: I-97, which we were supposed to be taking, heads southeast, and I-95, which we were on, heads southwest. I tried to give the bus driver the benefit of the doubt when I asked if we were taking this route to avoid traffic or get around an accident I wasn't aware of, but no. It turns out the driver had gotten confused with the highways and we had just spent the past half an hour driving in the opposite direction than where we needed to go. My bad field trip luck has to run out soon, right?

Wrong again.

Our bus turned around, got on the right highway, and we finally started making forward progress. I should probably add that our bus was the lead out of a total of three buses. The two buses following ours held the remaining three second grade classes, which had been split between the two buses. My class had the most students, so we were lucky enough to have our own bus.

I heard the bus driver's phone ring once before it connected to the Bluetooth device in his ear. I was only exposed to one side of the conversation, but it didn't sound promising. The bus driver hung up and informed me that one of the other buses was experiencing a mechanical issue so we needed to pull off the road to take a look. Since we had already added an extra hour to our trip from the highway confusion, quite a few students were requesting a bathroom break. The bus driver and I decided the nearby mall was a good place to stop.

We pulled into the parking lot outside of Sears, which suddenly increased the number of students needing a bathroom break from five to twenty-five. Shocker. I escorted my entire class of second graders into the optical department of Sears, where the bathrooms were located, and monitored them in the narrow hallway while dodging baffled looks from the nearby workers and customers.

Potty break accomplished, we returned to the bus to find nearly half the seats already occupied with students from the other second grade classes. I convened with my team teachers and learned that the third bus was completely broken down so we needed to combine the classes onto the two remaining buses. We smushed together in the seats, made room, and proceeded back to the highway, where we then sat in bumper-to-bumper traffic for nearly two hours. I wish I was kidding. It was the Friday before a massive beach event drawing over a quarter of a million attendees, and the bridge we needed to cross was part of the main route. Wonderful. I was prepared for a lot, but I don't think there's a large enough bookbag in the world to hold all the patience I needed for this field trip, which still wasn't over.

The next pit stop was at Domino's Pizza, which ordinarily would have excited me, but these circumstances put a damper on it. By the time we got across the bridge, it was 7:00 p.m. and our students were starving. Unlike at lunch, they weren't exaggerating this time. My principal had arranged for us to pick up several pizzas, enough to feed all the students, chaperones, and teachers, and quickly get back on the road. I used paper thin napkins to pass out slices of pizza, unfortunately none of them with pineapple, while our bus rolled down the highway, finally at a respectable pace.

During the entire ride home, I made continuous phone calls to families to update them with our estimated arrival time at school, which was originally scheduled for 3:30 p.m.

I called after our detour on the wrong highway. New ETA: 5:00 p.m.

I called after our Sears bathroom extravaganza and bus consolidation. New ETA: 6:00 p.m.

I called after our traffic standstill and impromptu pizza party. New ETA: 8:30 p.m.

We pulled into the school parking lot at 8:47 p.m. (that time is forever burned into my brain).

PLANS FIRST BUT FLEXIBILITY SECOND

Even as a self-proclaimed planning queen, there was only so much I could do to prepare for that field trip. I packed my bookbag with bandages, snacks, and potentially useful tools, but there was no way to predict we'd temporarily get lost, a bus would break down, and we'd have to stop for pizza. It hurt my organization-loving soul to let go of the perfectly planned field trip I had envisioned and embrace the chaos as it unfolded, but that was my only option.

In many ways, this field trip is representative of teaching as a whole. I will be the first person to tell you that planning is important. Whether it's planning for a field trip, upcoming lessons, assessments, or a fun classroom event, you need to spend time thinking things through before you start if you want to avoid complete disaster. It only takes one tube of glitter getting spilled all over your brand-new classroom carpet to make you realize how important it is to create a detailed plan when students are involved. Plans reduce uncertainty by helping you understand where you are going, increase efficiency by giving you steps to follow along the way, and facilitate your decision-making by keeping the focus on the end goal.

They're like a roadmap (or GPS since very few people use physical maps anymore). You locate where you are going or plug in your final destination and you can see exactly what roads you need to take to get there. It won't completely prevent you from getting lost, especially if you're like me and lack all natural sense of direction, but it certainly makes the journey easier.

Plans are a great guide. But unfortunately, that's all they are: a guide.

No matter how much time is spent preparing, a plan can never be perfect and adjustments will have to be made along the way. Just like when you follow a GPS, you may encounter unexpected road closures along the way or need to take an alternate route to avoid traffic.

When your plan no longer matches the current situation, it's easy to feel like you've failed. Your plan wasn't good enough. You aren't good enough. But when you understand that developing the flexibility to adjust the plan in these moments is far more important than creating a "perfect" plan to begin with, you become a more adaptable and resilient teacher.

There are many aspects of teaching that require flexibility.

One of the first lies in the grade level or subject area you teach. Before you get a classroom of your own, it's easy to get mentally attached to teaching a specific grade. You may have your classroom theme picked out and start tracking down resources for grade level content before you even have a teaching job. But the hiring process may serve as your first reality check when you realize that the position you get isn't in your dream grade level or even the subject you wanted to teach. Or, in rare cases, you might get swapped to a new grade level in the middle of the school year. Yes, that can happen. Not to mention, you'll probably be given a long list of rules to follow in your classroom such as not making any holes in the walls, which will completely derail your decoration plans.

You will also have to embrace flexibility when it comes to your lesson planning. You might have to teach a scripted curriculum with fidelity or you may have to collaborate closely with your team teachers to ensure you're all teaching lessons the same way and create consistency across your grade level. Chances are, these lessons won't fit your teaching style. It's also possible you could have to submit lesson plans on a weekly basis using a template or format that doesn't match the one you prefer using.

The need for flexibility increases significantly when it comes to the elements that involve students, such as teaching lessons and classroom management. There will be moments when your students aren't engaged and you will have to shift gears completely in the middle of a lesson to get their attention back. There will be other moments when your students are fully engaged but the information just isn't clicking the way you are teaching it. You might have to pause, reevaluate the lesson, consider how to present the content in a different way, and revisit the lesson the next day. You will also have times when students take a lesson in a completely different direction than what you had planned. These are my personal favorite moments because they drive real, authentic learning. Students may ask questions that spark a deep conversation, and you have to abandon your lesson plan in exchange for fueling their curiosity. It's a pretty good trade, in my opinion.

Classroom management is the ultimate flexibility test for teachers. Every single student you encounter over the course of your career will be different and come to you with unique needs. What works for one student may not work for another, and you have no choice but to continually adapt to the diverse needs in your classroom. You will try new strategies constantly and make small changes to the plan in place to meet students' physical, mental, emotional, social, and academic needs. As soon as you think you have found the perfect recipe for effective classroom management, something will change and turn it upside down. Guaranteed.

Understanding the need to be flexible is one thing, but actually practicing flexibility on a regular basis is harder than it looks, especially if your mind isn't properly warmed up to the idea. Thankfully, there are ways to stretch your thinking and increase your adaptability as a teacher.

LET GO OF YOUR ATTACHMENT

Before we even arrived at the museum on the day of the field trip, I had mentally drafted a minute-by-minute schedule for my group of students to follow. Eating lunch as soon as we set foot in the door at the bright and early time of 10:30 a.m. was not part of that schedule. But as I stood there in front of my very persuasive students (I think the puppy dog eyes played a role in their persuasion), I decided to abandon my original plan and try something different. The result? Eating lunch right away actually made a lot more sense. The small cafeteria was located right by the entrance, the lunches were taking up space in my bookbag and weighing it down, and it would prevent my students from asking the ever-popular question, "When is lunch?!"

If you become too attached to a plan, it can blind you from seeing any faults. You convince yourself that the original plan is the best plan and must be executed accordingly to achieve the best results and you become so stuck on one idea that you refuse to see the situation clearly. Once you let go of your attachment, you can identify the weak points in the original plan and objectively analyze the situation to see what needs to change. This clarity allows you to pivot before your plan falls apart completely.

The truth is, just because it's what you planned doesn't mean it's the best way. Situations change so plans have to change. Refusing to detach from the original plan only makes the journey more difficult, or in some cases, impossible. A GPS will reroute your trip to accommodate for traffic which may seem inconvenient, but staying on the original path just wastes time and may result in you getting stuck completely.

The plans you put in place as a teacher are no different. They are never set in stone and can always be adjusted, updated, or transformed to account for issues along the way. Stop a lesson if it is tanking. Pause an activity if you notice arguments. Abandon a classroom management strategy if it is causing more outbursts than it's preventing. Every second you continue following a failing plan is time you could have spent getting back on track.

PUT PEOPLE BEFORE YOUR PLANS

Making a pit stop at Domino's Pizza on the way home from the field trip was a bold choice. Most of the chaperones were annoyed with the decision to stop and made their disagreement very apparent. We had never planned to stop for food and this delayed our ETA even more. I was stuck between a rock and a hard place because I didn't want to upset the parents who had volunteered their time to help make this field trip possible but I also knew my students were hungry and unhappy.

Changing plans can be scary, especially as a new teacher when you already feel unsure about what you're doing in the first place. Not only is it difficult to let go of the original plan, but you might be nervous you'll get reprimanded by a superior, worried you'll be judged by other teachers, or concerned you'll look unprofessional to your students or their families. In some cases, these feelings are valid. But in most cases, these fears are fabricated and our minds are simply putting a negative spin on the possibilities. Either way, even the most flexible teachers experience moments of uncertainty when it comes to decision-making. You encounter situations where your heart and brain aren't on the same page and you feel torn trying to choose one to listen to.

In these moments, you have to bring yourself back to the "why" behind what you're doing. Why are you skipping certain lessons in the curriculum? Why are you using this book instead of that one? Why are you teaching a concept differently than the other teachers in your grade? Why are you stopping for pizza? You have to identify the reason behind the action you're taking. Okay, but how do you know your reasoning is sound? How do you know you are making the right choice, especially if others seem to disagree?

At the end of the day, people are always the most important. People are at the root of teaching and should always be at the forefront of your decision-making. Plans should never come before people.

Whether you change plans by choice or out of necessity, you have to keep the best interests of the people involved in mind from start to finish. For your students, this means prioritizing their physical, mental, emotional, social, and academic well-being, no matter what. Stopping for pizza was the best decision at that moment because it resulted in full bellies and happy students.

Putting people first might mean making drastic instructional decisions in the middle of a lesson to engage your students, make the content relevant, provide additional examples, or present the information in a new way. Jump on a chair to get their attention. Find a video of a skateboard trick to help them understand how many degrees are in a circle. Stop the lesson entirely if your students only become more confused by the second.

Pushing through an unengaging, confusing, or failing lesson just for the sake of staying on track with an arbitrary curriculum pacing guide doesn't serve your students. Shutting down productive conversations because "you don't have time" doesn't promote authentic learning. Be willing to alter a lesson to welcome teachable moments, make special connections, and answer curious questions. That's what's best for the most important people—your students.

Let's be clear: putting people before plans doesn't always guarantee perfect results. Mistakes will still be made and things will still go wrong. But, if something does go wrong, it's far better to justify your decision with intentions rooted in people than standards, rules, or other frivolous guidelines. In the end, "I did what I felt was best for my students" is a hard statement to argue with.

FOCUS ON YOUR CIRCLE OF CONTROL

Speaking of things going wrong, they will. A lot. Most of the time, things will go wrong because of no fault of your own.

Just like I had no control over the bus breaking down or the traffic building up before the bridge, you will encounter situations as a teacher that are completely outside of your circle of control.

On any given day in your classroom, there could be unexpected fire drills, random technology issues, or spontaneous behavior challenges. It never fails that these hiccups happen at the worst moments, like in the middle of a very important observation or when a parent is visiting your class. Yikes. In those moments, you feel embarrassed because it makes you look bad, frustrated because it isn't your fault, and annoyed because it doesn't seem fair.

Most plans have to change due to circumstances outside of your control, and dwelling on these can leave you feeling powerless and stuck. After a while, you get to the point where you aren't motivated to make any changes because it feels like they won't make a difference anyway. But by not making any changes, you're almost guaranteeing that the circumstances won't improve.

Shifting your focus from the overarching circumstances you can't control to the individual elements you can control leaves you feeling empowered and confident. It's a small but dynamic shift that can help you move forward in unexpected situations, which happen quite often in the world of teaching. Acknowledge that you can never control every aspect of a situation but you can always control your attitude about it. Remember that you can never control the actions of others but you can always control your reaction to them. Accept that you can never control the outcome of an event but you can always control the effort you choose to put in.

YOUR HOMEWORK

Make a list of things you can control. When you feel like chaos is taking over and you're losing control, it's helpful to have a list of things within your control as a reminder. Spend a few minutes brainstorming things within your circle of control and keep the list in a place you can easily reference it, like near your computer, in your lesson planner, or in a note-taking app on your phone. In times of frustration, look at your list and decide on changes you can make based on what's in your control. Here are a few ideas of things you can control to get your list started:

- Your attitude
- Responses to people and situations
- The effort you put in
- Boundaries you establish and maintain
- How you speak to yourself and others
- The actions you choose to take
- Your mindset
- How you treat other people
- The people you keep close
- How you handle your feelings

Adopt a mantra. A mantra is a word or phrase that gets repeated. Find a statement you can repeat to yourself when plans have to change. This statement should be short, simple, and remind you to be flexible. Here are a few example mantras you can steal for yourself:

- Plans are just a guide.
- Go with the flow.
- The best plans change.
- Bending is better than breaking.
- Flexibility results in stability.

Once you have selected your mantra, consider placing it somewhere visible so you are reminded of it often. You can write it on a sticky note or set it as the background of your computer desktop or phone. Repeat your mantra in your head or out loud when you feel yourself getting too attached to a specific plan.

Create and practice a flexibility routine. If you struggle with change, it is helpful to develop a routine you can follow each time things don't go according to plan. This routine should be short (five steps or less) but include steps that can help you embrace flexibility and avoid increased anxiety. Here is an example of steps that might be part of a flexibility routine:

1. Recognize plans need to change

2. Stop and breathe

3. Repeat your mantra

4. Consider your choices

5. Quickly pick the best one

Most of the time, the choices are very simple. You can either do this or do that. Instead of overcomplicating the decision, try to think about the options as black or white. For example, if your lesson is not going well, your choices are to keep teaching the lesson as it was planned or stop and make a change to the plans.

Take just the next step. If plans change, you don't have to create an entire new plan immediately. You're allowed to take it step by step and figure out the plan as you go. When you're feeling overwhelmed by the changes, take a second to focus on the easiest next step you can take. Let's say the internet loses connection in the middle of your lesson and the website you were using is no longer functioning. Your next step could be to:

- Pause the lesson and redirect students to another activity like reading a book (this will help occupy your students while you solve the problem or brainstorm your next steps).

- Call a team teacher to find out if they lost internet too (this will help you determine if the problem is schoolwide or just with your computer).

- Connect your computer to your phone's hotspot (this will help you potentially continue your lesson).

Rather than looking at the long road ahead and feeling lost without a roadmap, you can focus on just the next step you need to take to move forward.

Lean into spontaneity. A change of plans doesn't have to be a bad thing. Every new set of plans can be viewed as an opportunity to make a positive change. Rather than getting fixated on the fact that the original plan didn't work, focus on what could go right by being flexible. If it's a beautiful day outside and your students are staring out the window instead of engaging in your lesson, consider taking them outside to work. You can make an agreement with your students that they can have some extra recess time once they finish and submit their assignment. This might be a spontaneous change of plans, but could result in happier students who actually get their work done instead of distracted students who weren't being productive. Here are a few other ways you can be spontaneous as a teacher:

- Move the class to a new location (outside, the hallway, or another room in the school).
- Provide students with a random incentive (like free time).
- Allow students to take on the role of teacher.
- Follow student questions during a lesson.
- Incorporate current events.

With the amount of flexibility involved, teaching can feel a lot like performing a gymnastics routine. Just when you thought you were bending as much as humanly possible, something new happens and you're forced to bend a little further. But as long as you stay warm, your body adapts and you are somehow able to stretch a little bit more each time without breaking.

Flexibility is a skill that has to be practiced, strengthened, and maintained over time or else the ability slowly shrinks. You can train your flexibility as a teacher by letting go of your attachment to a particular set of plans, putting people first, and focusing on what you can control in the situation. The good news is teaching presents *plenty* of opportunities for you to practice. The even better news is that you can reduce the amount you have to bend in situations by anticipating potential problems and proactively implementing solutions before any stretching is required.

CHAPTER 5

What a Student Throws Up Must Come Down

Just like a baby learning to walk and talk, new teachers experience a lot of firsts. Most are heartwarming, like the first time a student draws you a picture or the first time you hear a student say, "You're the best teacher I've ever had!" (You might overhear them telling another teacher the exact same thing, but you can always pretend you didn't hear it.) Some are challenging, like the first time you wake up feeling nauseous in the middle of the night and have to write sub plans while heaving over the toilet in your bathroom. And others are downright disgusting, like the first time you get sneezed on, or worse, vomited on, by a student.

Since we're on the subject, let's revisit that glorious moment from my first day of teaching.

"I don't feel so good . . ."

The small boy who was bouncing down the hallway toward my classroom door just seconds ago was now standing directly in front of me, clenching his stomach with both arms. Since I remembered he was new to the school, much like myself, I assumed his queasy feeling stemmed from nerves.

"You're probably just feeling nervous because it's the first day of school. Here, let me show you your desk and help you unpa—"

Before I could finish my offer, what felt like the entire contents of his stomach were suddenly splattered down the front of my legs and a puddle of vomit formed at my feet.

It was one of those moments that felt like it was happening in slow motion, but yet I still couldn't prevent it or move out of the way fast enough. The damage was done.

The good news? My first experience with student vomit was out of the way. The bad news? My shoes were soaked. Conveniently, I was wearing closed-toed shoes but the opening in the back unfortunately allowed some to seep inside. I'll spare you the rest of the vile details as I'm sure your imagination is already running wild.

There was more good news. This was immediately followed by another first, but this time, a heartwarming one. The boy looked up at me with apologetic eyes and said, "I'm sorry . . . you can borrow my shoes if they fit you."

After assuring him it was okay, my brain went into hyperdrive trying to decide what to do next. I started walking toward the sink in the back of my classroom to retrieve some paper towels, but suddenly remembered the health and safety training modules I had completed online a week earlier. Teachers weren't supposed to come in contact with any form of student-produced fluids without gloves, which of course I didn't have. I would have to call a custodian to take care of the cleanup, which now included the footprints of vomit that tracked halfway to the sink and back. Besides, the thin, brown paper towels that were stocked in our classrooms had a tendency to push messes around more than they absorbed them so it was probably for the best.

Before I could make it to my phone to call for a custodian, it hit me that I was missing a pretty vital step. I needed to send the boy to the nurse first. I shuffled some papers around my desk desperately hoping to find some nurse passes even though I had no memory of ever receiving any, but as expected, my search came up empty. I assumed the pass was just a formality and ushered him out the door empty handed.

"Wait, take the trash can with you!" Round one might have ended up on the floor but if there happened to be a round two, I wanted him to be prepared.

I quickly called the custodian to initiate the clean-up process, used the nearly worthless paper towels to soak up as much vomit from my shoes as possible, and resumed greeting my new students, slightly smellier than before.

After dodging the mess on the floor and walking some students to their seats, I turn around to see the same boy standing at my doorway, holding the trash can by his side.

"She told me to come back and get a pass."

The only school-appropriate words circulating around my brain were, "You've got to be kidding me." I called the nurse to explain the situation and sent the boy on his way again, fingers crossed that this was the last time. Just then, the custodian arrived with a cart full of supplies to tackle the job. He sprinkled some kind of magical powder that instantly began absorbing the mess and smell, which captivated my students' attention long enough for me to regain my composure before escorting my class to art.

There was one casualty that day. The trashcan I sent with the boy to the nurse, the only trashcan I had for my classroom at the time, never returned. It must have been sacrificed to the "first day of teaching" gods as a desperate plea to make the rest of the school year much easier.

ANTICIPATE AND DISSIPATE

You probably guessed it but the sacrificial trashcan was not enough to make the rest of my first year of teaching any less difficult. My year would go on to be filled with countless other firsts that I learned how to navigate in real time, just like every other new teacher.

If you're lucky, these firsts will space themselves out and the challenging and disgusting ones will sandwich themselves between the heartwarming ones. But most likely, these firsts will all be thrown at you, or thrown up on you, when you least expect it.

The good news is that the first time is always the hardest time. The process is always unclear until you have been through something at least once. Since you don't know how the situation should play out, you're attempting to figure it out as you go, which sets you up to make mistakes. But once you gain experience, you can make better decisions and the process gets easier.

The bad news is that teaching is filled with *a lot* of firsts.

The first new student who joins your class in the middle of the year without any warning.

The first angry phone call from a parent that leaves you in tears and questioning your career choice.

The first loose tooth you help a student pull out because they ask you to.

The first surprise observation from an administrator that you're completely unprepared for.

The first real diamond ring a student brings to school and gives to a crush that you have to get back and contact home about (yes, that really happened to me).

Every one of these firsts makes your job feel harder than it is because you're trying to maneuver through uncharted teaching territory.

But, there's more good news. While you can never avoid the firsts, you can anticipate them happening and dissipate some of the uncomfortable feelings.

Even if it didn't happen on the first day of school, I was bound to experience a student throwing up in my classroom at some point in my teaching career. It wasn't a complete surprise. Obviously, it was surprising that it happened within the first fifteen minutes of my first day of teaching, but it wasn't an unpredictable situation (like the one you'll read about in the next chapter). I should have thought about how I would react and had a plan ready, since it was a question of when it would happen, not if.

Most firsts you'll experience as a new teacher are predictable. You can anticipate them, which means you can proactively prepare for them. Whether it's students getting sick in class, managing behavior problems, or waking up ill and needing a substitute, you can take action in advance to make the experience easier.

FORECAST THE FUTURE

If you're going on a trip to a place you've never been before, it's a good idea to check the weather so you know what to pack in your suitcase. You will want to have a jacket or umbrella if it's going to rain, gloves if it's going to snow, and short sleeve shirts if it's going to be sunny. The forecast may change slightly, but at least your wardrobe selection will make sense for the typical weather in that location and season.

Much like the weather, you can anticipate events you'll experience as a teacher based on patterns, historical data, and common sense. You know that student behavior tends to become more erratic toward the end of the school year just like you know the temperature tends to be warmer the closer you get to the equator. You've experienced it yourself as a student, you've probably heard other teachers talk about it, and it just makes sense. You can use this behavior forecast to take action in advance and help mitigate the negative effects just like you can use a weather forecast to pick the clothes you'll wear for the day.

When it comes to the aspects of teaching that worry you, such as student behavior, angry parents, parent-teacher conferences, or observations, most of the stress you experience stems from feeling unprepared. You aren't sure what to expect, the best way to handle it, or what happens if you do something wrong.

But thankfully, a lot of these situations are easy to anticipate either through your own foresight or the insight of others. If you take time to think through these situations and consider the different scenarios before they occur for the first time, you can predict what the challenges might be, what could go wrong, how you would react, and what materials you might need. It takes time and effort to examine these possibilities, but the peace of mind you gain from feeling prepared is well worth it. Then, you can supplement your lack of experience by enlisting the help of others. Ask other teachers you know, find a mentor you can consult, or do research in these areas so you know what to expect and can be prepared properly.

Tackling all the firsts that come with teaching is hard, but a lot of stress and detrimental mistakes can be avoided through anticipation and proactive actions. Rather than waiting for these inevitable moments to arise, ask yourself what you can do now to make it an easier experience later. These are the actions that your future self will thank you for. A few examples include:

- Adding scheduled events like conference days or field trips to your calendar and setting reminders

- Asking your coworkers questions like, "What does this usually look like?" or "What should I do to prepare for this?"

- Studying the forms, documents, and guidelines provided by your school or district for various events like evaluations, conferences, and field trips

- Searching online for examples from other teachers

- Saving ideas to reference in the future

- Collecting materials in advance

- Having a backup plan for when things go wrong

CONSTRUCT A KIT

On the evening before my first day of teaching, my then-boyfriend and now-husband, Billy, gave me a gift. He wanted to ease my nerves and help me feel more prepared for this brand-new endeavor so he presented me with what he referred to as a "teacher survival kit." Inside the box was a collection of small personal care items, each with a cute and metaphorical purpose. There was a mini stick of deodorant so I didn't sweat the small stuff, a tiny lint roller so I could dust myself off if I fell, and lots of chocolate so I could eat my feelings. The last one was more literal than metaphorical, but still appreciated nonetheless.

Unfortunately, the teacher survival kit didn't include an extra pair of shoes that I desperately could have used on my first day of school, but it did make me feel more confident going into the day.

Aside from chocolate, kits are a teacher's best friend. By including items, materials, and resources you might need to prevent or solve anticipated problems, you can significantly increase your chances of success in any given situation. Taking time to prepare kits that can be easily grabbed and put to use in your classroom makes your life easier and sets you up to thrive.

Following are a few kits I believe every teacher should keep in their classroom. They don't have to be created all at once, but strive to construct them sooner rather than later so you can reap the benefits as soon as possible.

Teacher Kit

- Change of clothes
- Personal hygiene items
- Makeup
- Snacks
- Battery charging pack (for phones or other small electronics)
- Cash and change

Beginning-of-the-Year Kit

- Scissors
- Stapler
- Staple remover
- Tape
- Cleaning wipes
- Duster
- Items for your desk
- Name tags
- Beginning of the year paperwork
- Copies for the first week of school

New Student Kit

(Tip: print a few extras of all the materials you prepare for your students at the beginning of the year and assemble a few of these kits at the same time.)

- Information for parents
- Forms to be completed
- Small welcome treat or gift
- Name tag
- Supply labels
- List of routines to teach the student
- List of important information to share with the student
- List of documents to update with your new roster

Emergency Kit

■ Student roster (be sure to update this several times throughout the year)

■ Family contact information (same as above)

■ Small first aid kit

■ Flashlight and extra batteries

■ Battery charging pack (for phones or other small electronics)

■ Nonperishable snacks

Substitute Kit

■ Sub binder with information about your classroom, students, and routines (be sure to update this several times throughout the year as your roster, schedule, or procedures change)

■ Emergency sub plans (ideally two-to-five days' worth that include review activities so they can be used at any time)

■ Copies of any papers or activities needed for the emergency sub plans

■ Treat for the substitute (optional but always appreciated)

Lesson Kit

This should be a fully planned and prepared lesson that can be used at any time if another lesson fails, you experience technology problems, or something else unexpected occurs. Guidelines to consider:

■ No technology is needed.

■ All material is review (no new concepts are being introduced).

- Minimal materials are needed (only use basic supplies like paper and pencil).
- Incorporate different subject areas, if possible.

Field Trip Kit

- Clipboard and pen
- Small first aid kit
- Tissues
- Hand sanitizer
- Wet wipes
- Nonperishable snacks
- Lip balm
- Battery charging pack (for phones or other small electronics)
- Weather attire (umbrella, poncho, sunglasses, etc.)
- Cash and change
- Plastic bag or trash bag

Calm Down Kit

This should be accessible to students, with permission, and include items they can use independently to handle their emotions. Here are a few ideas of items to include:

- Sand timers
- Fidgets
- Books
- Feeling identification chart
- Printable calm down strategies

Student Birthday Kit

This should include any treats or items you want to give students for their birthday. You can save time by preparing enough for your entire class at the beginning of the year. Here are a few ideas of items to include:

- Certificates
- Pencils
- Erasers
- Candy

WATCH AND LEARN

Think back to the first time you drove a car. You were most likely excited for the new experience (and anticipated freedom it would bring), but also insanely nervous. When you first got behind the wheel, you probably didn't know how to position your mirrors correctly or the appropriate amount of force to put on the gas and brake pedals, but thankfully you had an experienced driver in the passenger seat next to you who could guide you through the process.

All of the firsts you experience as a teacher are scary, but you can rest assured that although they are firsts for you, they are not firsts for the world of teaching. All of the situations you try to prepare for have already been encountered by so many teachers before you and you are fortunate enough to have the opportunity to learn from their experiences.

Use this to your advantage. When you aren't sure how to get your students to walk quietly in the hallway, find strategies other teachers have used. When your students aren't understanding a specific topic, find resources other teachers have created. When you wake up sick in the middle of the night, look online for a set of sub plans that have already been written so you can go back to bed.

You shouldn't recreate the wheel or struggle in silence when the solutions to your problems already exist. You just have to find them. This includes observing other teachers in your building, searching online for answers to your questions, and collaborating with those around you to gain new perspectives and ideas.

Teachers before you have walked so you can run. Don't let their efforts go to waste.

YOUR HOMEWORK

Choose one thing you feel unprepared for. You probably have an infinitely expanding list of things stressing you out in your head, and most of the stress comes from feeling unprepared. Take a look at your calendar or brainstorm upcoming events and pick the one you feel the least prepared for. This might include:

- Unplanned lessons for the next day, week, or month
- Scheduled observation (or a surprise observation you know is coming soon)
- Parent-teacher conferences
- Field trip
- Meeting (IEP meeting, 504 meeting, department meeting, faculty meeting, committee meeting, etc.)
- New curriculum to start implementing

Write down the potential problems and pair each with a solution. Go through the situation in your head like a movie and anticipate what could go wrong or potential issues that could arise. For each problem you think of, decide how you will handle it or find a coordinating solution. If you feel unprepared for upcoming parent-teacher conferences, your potential problems and solutions might look something like this:

Problem: You're worried you'll forget what you wanted to discuss about a student.

Solution: Create a conference sheet for each student with data points, items to discuss, and questions to ask.

Problem: A parent interrupts a conference you're having with another family.

Solution: Create and post a sign for your door to tell families when a conference is in session.

Problem: A parent asks you for resources and you have nothing to give them.

Solution: Prepare a variety of printables, pamphlets, and websites you can present to families during the conference and offer to send a follow-up email with any additional resources you don't have on hand.

Create a coordinating kit. Gather all the materials you would need to implement these solutions, plus anything else that comes to mind that might be useful for the situation. For example, your conference kit might include:

- "Conference in session" sign
- Copies of blank sign-in sheets

- Notebook and pen

- Copies of blank conference sheets to fill out for each student

- Folders to hold and organize all the papers for each conference (conference sheet, work samples, copies of missing assignments, documentation of behavior problems, etc.)

- Printable resources for families to take

- Mints or treats to have available for families

- Coloring pages or games to occupy students or siblings who attend

- Tissues (conferences can sometimes get emotional)

Keep all of the materials together in a box, bin, or bag and find a location to store this kit so it is ready to go when you need it.

Create "go-to" lists. These are reference lists of things you know work in a situation. Your lists can include things you've personally tried but also ideas you've gotten from other teachers. You can keep these lists in a notebook or in your phone so you can look through them when you feel unprepared in a situation and get ideas of things to try. Here are a few "go-to" lists you should consider making:

Go-to student celebrations: These are simple ways you can make students feel special and successful in your class. When you get super busy, it's easy to forget these small gestures so this list of ideas can help remind you to celebrate your students and their hard work. These are my favorite celebrations that are completely free:

- Class cheers. Students get to pick a cheer for the class to perform for them (my personal favorite is the cheese grater . . . you hold up a fist and say, "Here's the cheese," then you hold up an open hand and say, "Here's the grater," and then rub them together and say, "You're great, great, great, great . . .").

■ Celebration tunnel. Your class forms two lines facing each other and high five or cheer for the student running (safely) down the middle.

■ Positive phone call or email home. This one is pretty basic but students *love* to be involved in the process so let them join you on the phone call or help you write the email (it can be super motivational for other students in the class to see this happening as well).

Go-to time fillers: These are quick and easy games or activities you can use at any time without any prep. You can use these if you arrive somewhere early, like an assembly, have something unexpected happen and need to kill time, or just have a few extra minutes after a lesson ends. These are a few games my students always loved:

■ Quiet game. Students stand in a silent line while one student steps out of line, chooses a student who isn't talking, taps them on the shoulder, and then trades places.

■ Twenty-one. Students take turns sequentially counting up to three numbers at a time (the first student might say "one two," the second student might say "three," and then the third student might say "four five six") until someone lands on twenty-one and is out.

■ Detective. One student volunteers to leave the room or look away while a "leader" is selected (the rest of the students must imitate the leader's movements) and then has three guesses to figure out who the leader is by watching the movements closely.

Go-to responses: These are things you can say when you're trying to get your class back on track during a lesson, diffusing an angry student or family member, comforting an upset student or family member, or keeping a boundary in place. Here are a few of my favorites:

- "We have a lot of fish to fry and only one skillet!"
- "I hear what you're saying. What would you like from me at this moment?"
- "I'm so sorry that happened. How can I bring a little sunshine to your day?"
- "That's not going to work for me."

Each time you try something that works in a given situation, add it to your list so you don't forget about it in the future. Over time, you will build your own database of ideas and strategies you know will be successful.

In addition to flexible gymnasts ready to bend in any given direction at a moment's notice, teachers also have become fortune tellers who are able to predict the future within their classroom. Learning how to anticipate potential issues that could arise and proactively working to prevent them or take action immediately as they occur can help you feel in control. This feeling of security is important when you're in a profession where so much can feel out of your control, and these feelings result in stress and overwhelm.

But, you can read every teaching book, attend all the professional development seminars, and *still* not be prepared for every situation. Some of the circumstances teaching throws at you won't come with a prepared kit or the wisdom of an experienced teacher, so you have to adopt a solution-driven mindset to overcome these obstacles.

CHAPTER 6

When Teaching Gives You Stress, Go to Recess

Starting a new school year is a lot like baking a cake using a new recipe. You understand the process of baking and the steps are the same as usual, but the slight differences in ingredients and measurements can have a drastic effect on the overall quality and taste of the cake. As a teacher, your class is the cake, your students are the ingredients, and you are the baker.

Every new group of students you welcome into your class presents a fresh and interesting dynamic. Some groups of students are overly chatty, others easily get off task during lessons, and then there are the groups who bicker constantly like siblings. There are classes that seem like a recipe for disaster, until you find the right combination of ingredients to create a balanced taste. You may have to experiment with the measurements, the order in which ingredients are mixed, and the time in the oven, but you can always find a way to produce a delicious cake with the ingredients you are given.

During my third year of teaching, my baking skills were put to the test. My particular group of students were talkative, unfocused, and quarrelsome, and I was struggling to successfully manage and produce the cooperative class I envisioned. I decided to tackle the recipe one step at a time, starting with our time on the carpet. My students sat together on the large, rectangular carpet in the front of my classroom to participate in mini lessons on a daily basis. They were masters at sitting with their legs crossed and their hands in their lap to prevent fingers from getting stepped on, but there was one glaring issue. My students were blurters.

It was as if every thought that entered their brain, regardless of relevancy or importance, immediately exited through their mouth without any prior warning. There was no hand raising. There was no waiting to get called on. There were only random blurts of thoughts, comments, and questions. What started as slightly humorous (because having a student call out, "Did you know a cucumber can become a pickle but a pickle can't become a cucumber?" in the middle of a lesson *is* funny) quickly became frustrating beyond belief.

I had to find a way to prevent my students from blurting out on the carpet, so I did what most new teachers would do. I turned to the internet.

I settled on a strategy appropriately titled "Blurt Beans." Basically, you would give each student a bean to hold before sitting down on the carpet. I had seen a variety of beans used by other teachers from kidney beans to lima beans, so I chose the cheapest option of dry beans at the store, which happened to be small pinto beans. Any student who blurted out during the lesson had to forfeit their bean but any student who still had a bean left in their hand at the end of carpet time got to add their bean to a jar. Once the beans in the jar reached a certain level, the entire class earned an agreed-upon prize like extra recess time or a popcorn party. The concept was simple. Fewer blurts equals more beans in the jar, which means the prize is earned sooner.

It sounded great in theory.

I introduced the idea to my students and they were sold. It took a few days of practice, but the blurt frequency began to decrease as the number of beans in the prize jar increased. We were well on our way to blurt-free carpet time, and I was thrilled.

In hindsight, I should have known that it was a little too easy.

I was in the middle of a reading lesson on the front carpet when I suddenly heard a student frantically yell out, "It's stuck!" I didn't have to ask what was stuck. I already knew. It was the bean.

My brain immediately began cycling through the possible locations the bean could be stuck. Mouth. Nose. Other small openings on the body. Some options were certainly better than others so I grimaced as I asked my follow-up question.

Me: "Where is it stuck?"

The student: "In my ear!"

Okay. Not the best option, but definitely not the worst option. I'll take it. I proceeded with the next logical question.

Me: "Why was the bean in your ear?"

The student: "I was doing a magic trick!"

Reasonable. I didn't ask for an explanation or details but I got a clear understanding of the failed disappearing act I was witnessing. This student probably wouldn't sell out magic shows any time soon, but it made sense.

It's no secret that students tend to exaggerate things. They love to make situations out to be more exciting, outrageous, and dire than they truly are so I assumed "stuck" was a slight embellishment on the actual state of the bean.

I walked over to the student and my eyes locked on the small, brown pinto bean wedged in the crevice of his left ear. I tried to gently dislodge it using the tip of my finger but quickly realized "stuck" was not an exaggeration. The bean didn't budge.

It became apparent that I had to send this student to the nurse, but deciding what to write on the pass was a little more difficult. Simply writing "bean stuck in ear" was an open invitation for a series of follow-up questions, much like the ones I had just finished asking the student, so I opted to call the nurse and explain the situation instead. After letting out a small giggle, the nurse told me to send the student up to her office and she would see what she could do.

Success! I received a phone call just a few minutes later informing me that the bean had been removed and I finally let out a massive sigh of relief. While on the phone, the nurse then asked me if I wanted the bean returned with the student in a small plastic baggie, as if it were a lost tooth that deserved celebration. Of course I answered yes.

Within a few seconds, the student returned enthusiastically, skipping through my doorway and victoriously held up his plastic bean baggie for the rest of the class to see. At this point, my stress levels were far too high to continue my lesson (plus, I think we *all* had learned some valuable lessons that day) so I decided to award my students their extra recess time a little prematurely.

There was one final hurdle to cross: I had to inform this student's family of the incident. Surely, it was not in my best interest to let this student personally recount the events when he got home without first clarifying some of the details.

I dialed the phone number and started practicing my concise recap of events while it rang.

Bean was in his hand. Bean was in his ear. Bean was stuck. Bean was removed. Student is okay. Bada bean, bada boom. No, wait. Scratch that last part.

His mom's reaction is a little bit of a blur, but I do remember something along the lines of, "That sounds like something he would do," being sandwiched between bursts of laughter. She was not at all surprised, and was just thankful it wasn't something worse.

In case you're wondering, the Blurt Beans were promptly retired after that day and I still have a good laugh with the student's family when the Facebook memory pops up each year.

THERE'S A SOLUTION FOR EVERY PROBLEM

Removing a bean from that student's ear was not part of my lesson plan that day. It was a unique situation I never could have anticipated, but it was still a problem I had to tackle.

By my third year of teaching, I thought the hard stuff was over. I thought the uncomfortable situations I didn't know how to handle were a thing of the past and I had finally gained enough experience for teaching to be smooth sailing.

Boy, was I wrong.

As you embark on your first year of teaching, you expect to encounter problems. Everything is brand new and you knew it would be hard. You see every problem as an opportunity to learn and grow and you confidently believe you'll come out on the other side stronger, wiser, and more qualified to handle what teaching throws at you in the future.

And you do.

But a few years go by, and there are still situations you don't know how to handle. You feel like this should be easier by now. You feel like you shouldn't still be making mistakes. You feel broken and defeated because you still have moments when you don't know what you're doing.

You feel like you're the only teacher still struggling.

And you're not.

No one ever has all the answers, especially in the world of teaching. There's no magical one-size-fits-all approach that works for every person in every situation.

Trying to avoid problems as a teacher is like trying to avoid sand at the beach. It's impossible.

You can read every teaching book, attend every seminar, and consult every expert in an effort to be as prepared as possible but you will still encounter obstacles along the way.

You can respond to these obstacles in two ways:

1   You can focus on the problems.

2   You can focus on the solutions.

If you're covered in sand at the beach, you can choose to focus on how uncomfortable it is or you can find ways to get the sand off. One leaves you feeling discouraged and negative (and probably a little itchy) while the other leaves you feeling hopeful and positive. It's your choice.

When you encounter problems in the world of teaching, which is often, you can choose to dwell on how frustrating they are or you can find ways to solve them. Focus on being a problem solver instead of a problem dweller.

Instead of trying to avoid problems like sand at the beach, feel confident that you can find or create a solution to any problem that does come up, even if you weren't prepared for it.

You can find a solution for every problem or you can find a problem for every solution, and the choice you make has a direct impact on your happiness as a teacher.

ADJUST YOUR ZOOM

If the choice is that simple, why are there so many people who choose to dwell on their problems? Why are there so many teachers complaining in the teacher's lounge, in staff meetings, or on social media? Why don't they just shift their focus from the problem to the solution?

As human beings, we are designed to look for the path of least resistance. We naturally want to take the easy way out and avoid friction at all costs. Finding a solution to a problem involves friction. It requires effort, especially when the solution isn't obvious or floating at the surface.

Simply put, it's easier to complain about problems than it is to solve them.

As you begin to challenge this mindset actively and shift your focus to solutions, you'll find they aren't always so easy to come by. Some solutions will be common sense, like setting an alarm on your phone to remind you to take your students to lunch if you keep forgetting, but others will remain a mystery and you may even convince yourself that a solution for the problem doesn't exist. These are the moments you have to adjust your zoom.

Like the lens of a camera, your perspective of a situation can be zoomed in or out.

By zooming in, you're diving deep and taking a closer look at the finite details of a situation. This allows you to address the root cause of a problem instead of merely responding to the symptoms. Start with the problem you see at the surface and work backward. Keep asking yourself, "But why is this happening?" and find specific answers until you are able to notice an ongoing pattern or an initial trigger that can be targeted with a solution.

By zooming out, you're examining the bigger picture and maybe even consulting those not directly involved in the situation to gain a wider perspective. As your view broadens, consider the simplest solutions first. For example, maybe the behavior problems are surfacing because you stopped being consistent with your expectations, spring break is approaching and students are burnt out, or it's a full moon (ask any teacher and they will tell you that behavior problems around full moons are *real*). A simple solution would be tightening up your consistency. Then, ask yourself if the problem is even worth fixing. Is the problem temporary? Can it be ignored? Is the juice worth the squeeze? (Which in this case means: Is the effort it takes to solve the problem worth the outcome?)

As you adjust your zoom, make sure the size of the solution matches the size of the problem. Most problems you encounter will not require you to go back to the drawing board and formulate a solution from scratch. Especially after zooming in or out, you can just make small adjustments to your current practices to regain focus of the problem at hand.

START WITH AN IMPERFECT SOLUTION

Another reason it's difficult for people to adopt a solution-focused mindset is that it requires letting go of perfection. For most perfectionists, myself included, it's scary to try and fail at something, so they would rather not try at all.

When trying to solve a problem, you might not find the exact solution right away. You may need to ask for advice or use trial and error to find the right fit, and that involves accepting imperfection. But starting with an imperfect solution to a problem is always more effective than never trying to solve it at all.

But, the best problem solvers don't create problems for others as part of their solution process. If you do have to reach out for help along the way, do so with a solution ready to suggest, even if it's a messy solution.

If you're going to meet with an administrator to discuss a problem you've noticed in your school, offer a potential way to improve it. Maybe you've observed students running to their classrooms in the morning and want to suggest stationing staff members in the hallway to greet them and make sure they move through the hallway safely.

If you're going to contact a parent with an academic concern about a student, be prepared to share what you have already tried and what you want to try next. Maybe a student is struggling to read fluently and you've tried encouraging them to use a whisper phone when reading to hear their own voice but want to try meeting with them weekly to practice some fluency passages.

These suggestions aren't guaranteed solutions, but they help take the stress off the other individuals you are involving in the problem. This makes it easier for them to collaborate with you to solve the problem, and, as I mentioned, people are attracted to the path of least resistance.

As you navigate through various solutions, remember that done is better than perfect and you can continue adjusting if needed. Don't worry, if the problem doesn't get sufficiently solved, it will resurface and you'll have another opportunity to conquer it.

LEARN FROM YOUR MISTAKES

Dwelling on problems is also easier than accepting responsibility for their occurrence. Many of the problems we face are a direct result of something we either did or didn't do, which is hard to admit. But the faster you can recognize and accept that a problem you are experiencing is a consequence of your actions, the faster you can learn from your mistakes and make changes.

Mistakes are inevitable but the future problems they cause don't have to be. You can never go back and change what happened in the past, but you can make adjustments when you recognize the trajectory is headed toward disaster.

So how exactly do you prevent mistakes from being repeated in the future? You learn from them.

Learning starts with reflection. When something goes wrong or you make a mistake, take time to consider what went well and what needs to be improved. Do a little homework to find or create possible solutions to the problems you identify.

Learning continues through implementation and adjustment. You have to try the potential solutions, monitor how the outcome changes, and then make small changes as needed until you achieve the desired outcome.

Finally, your learning is solidified through documentation. Write down the solution you found. Take pictures of artifacts so you don't forget. Record data to share with others.

Again, a majority of the problems you face in the profession are universal. If you are struggling with something, it's likely another teacher is, too. When you find a creative solution to a common problem, share it with the teaching community so others can benefit from your efforts. That's one of the easiest ways to be part of the solution instead of the problem in the world of education.

YOUR HOMEWORK

Reflect on a recent teaching experience that didn't go as expected. Think of a lesson that bombed, a negative interaction with a student, or unfavorable feedback you received. Fold a piece of paper to form two columns and write down what went well during the experience on one side and write down what didn't go well on the other side. The things that didn't go well can help you identify the existing problems and the things that did go well can be used as inspiration for the solutions since these are your current strengths.

Choose one problem to solve. Look through the things that didn't go well and identify one corresponding problem. You might need to adjust your zoom by looking at the bigger picture or taking a deeper dive to identify the root cause of a problem. Keep in mind that sometimes solving one problem will automatically fix others. For example, solving the problem of students not transitioning between tasks efficiently can reduce behavior issues that arise from not having enough time to get through content. Choose the problem that will have the biggest overall impact on the situation.

Find a solution. It's nearly impossible that you are the first person to ever encounter this problem so a viable solution most likely already exists. Do your research by asking other teachers or searching online and find at least one potential solution to try (although it might be helpful to have backup plans). If you are trying to find ways for students to transition between tasks more quickly, you could try any combination of the following solutions:

- Time the transition and set a goal together of a target time to work toward.

- Play "beat the clock" and have students try to transition under an allotted time.

- Post a visual timer for students to see as they transition.

- Play the chorus of a song that is the same length as the ideal transition time.

- Put a student in charge of monitoring the transition each time.

- Make it a competition between the teacher and students (the teacher gets a point if the transition is too slow and the students get a point if the transition is under an allotted time).

Remember, it doesn't have to be a perfect solution. Something is better than nothing.

Implement the solution. Put your plan into play immediately. Don't wait for a new week, new month, or new marking period to make changes. Commit to trying the solution you've picked as soon as you can. Gather and prepare the materials you might need so you have no excuses for not implementing it.

Document the solution. You want to make sure you "cover your tracks," so to speak. If the problem continues to grow, you want proof you took action and it will be helpful to reference things you have already tried that didn't work. Plus, if you reach out for additional support from an administrator or mentor teacher, you might be asked to share data related to the issue. This is where your documentation comes in. Here are a few ways you can document the solution you implement:

- Make a note of the changes you made on that day in your lesson planner (for example: introduced a new seating chart).

- Write the behavior management strategies you implemented on an individual student data sheet and note the dates or specific times (for example: introduced a new incentive system using stickers).

- Keep track of progress on a clipboard (for example: recording the time it takes your students to transition each day).

- Send an email to families to notify them of changes being made in your classroom (for example: letting families know about a new assignment redo policy you will be implementing).

It's better to document these changes and not end up needing the documentation than it is to need it and not have it.

Adjust as needed. You might get it right on the first try, but chances are your solution will need adjustment along the way. First, consider your consistency. It's possible your solution just needs more consistent implementation over a longer period of time for noticeable changes to occur. If this is the case, you can use a simple habit tracker to note your consistency and hold yourself accountable.

But, if you find that the solution you implement escalates the problem or does not make any notable impact, continue to make small changes until the problem is solved appropriately. These changes might include adjusting the frequency, intensity, or delivery of your actions. For example, if you display a visual timer when students transition from math centers, you might consider displaying the same visual timer during all transitions that occur throughout the day, like getting ready for lunch or preparing for dismissal.

If there's one thing that's guaranteed in teaching, it's that there will always be new obstacles to tackle, even for the most experienced teachers. Some of these obstacles will be the first of many occurrences and the solutions you develop will serve you when the problem arises again in the future. Some of these obstacles, like removing a bean from a student's ear, will be once-in-a-teaching-career occurrences that, hopefully, never resurface.

Still, adopting a solution-focused mindset will help you navigate these situations with confidence instead of apprehension. The less time you spend dwelling on these unpredictable and unavoidable problems, the more time you can spend fostering a memorable and engaging learning environment for your students, which in turn helps you move one step closer to the teacher you desire to become.

CHAPTER 7

You Can Be Saved by the Bells and Whistles

Everyone copes with stress in different ways. You might eat a snack, take a nap, read a book, spend time with friends, take a bath, or, if you're anything like me, exercise. I started running in high school with cross country and track, but transitioned to marathon training when I was in college. With the goal of graduating with my bachelor's degree in only three years, my stress levels were high, which meant my runs got longer, so the transition into marathon running made perfect sense.

I ran my first marathon during the fall of my third year of college. At the time, I was student-teaching at a local elementary school one day a week while completing my last semester of undergrad classes before my full-time internship began in January. This means my brain was constantly in teacher mode. I was always scanning the room and taking mental notes of things I wanted to incorporate into my own teaching in the fall. Every event I attended, place I visited, and person I talked to was an opportunity to get ideas for my future classroom, and I was taking full advantage.

When you finish a marathon, the volunteers on the sidelines place a medal over your head, wrap you in a foil blanket to stay warm, and swiftly guide you to a celebration village filled with tents and booths for various vendors. This is where you can meet your family and friends to take pictures and indulge in plenty of snacks and beverages of choice. As I wobbled into the celebration village (I had just finished a marathon after all), teacher mode was activated and I began scanning the field for ideas. My eyes locked on a bell.

At one booth, there was a metal bell, about the size of my head, set up with a sign that read, "Ring me if you set a PR today!" A PR is a personal record, and since this was my first marathon, I technically had set a new PR. As I reached up and gave the bell a hearty ring, it dawned on me. I can use this in my classroom.

I wasn't quite sure how, but I knew I could incorporate this concept into my teaching. There's something about ringing a bell loud enough for everyone else to hear as a way to signal an accomplishment that is incredibly motivating. I knew my future students would love it.

Fast-forward to the following fall when I began my first year of teaching. When you visit your classroom for the first time, you never know exactly what you're walking into. It's possible that your classroom is entirely empty, besides the desks, chairs, and other furniture pieces that belong to the school, but it's also possible that you are inheriting a classroom from a retired teacher who decided to leave anything and everything for you to sift through. My classroom was somewhere in the middle.

I was taking over a classroom from a teacher who moved grade levels, so it wasn't completely jam packed with stuff, but there were plenty of resources and materials left behind. One of the best pieces of advice I received going into my first year of teaching was to hold on to these materials for a year, figure out what I needed or would use during that time, and then get rid of anything I hadn't touched. This meant I had to organize and store everything that was already in my classroom before I started bringing in my own items. Most teachers would probably find this overwhelming and stressful, but I was in heaven.

My parents volunteered to help me sort through the miscellaneous containers, cabinets, and drawers to get things organized before the school year started. Thankfully, I got my organization genes from my mom and my dad . . . well, he was really good at moving furniture around the room. I remember each of them holding up random items and asking, "What is this for?" and my answer was usually, "I don't know . . . ask me at the end of the year." I was just praying that I would actually figure it out along the way.

We decided to throw away the papers and worksheets that were so faded you could barely make out what they said along with the old, stained transparency sheets because, fortunately, my classroom did not have an overhead projector (if you have no idea what that is, just Google it). While I continued to rummage through the drawers, my mom held up a small, gold bell with a black handle she found in a cabinet and asked if I wanted to keep it. The memory of my first marathon immediately came flooding back and I let out an enthusiastic, "*Yes!*"

The hand bell secured a spot on the corner of my desk until I could brainstorm a creative way to use it. My students would often ask, "What's that bell for?" and I would reply, "You'll find out soon!" but in reality, I had nothing.

After spending a few weeks thinking, I finally settled on using the bell as an incentive for my students to match or beat their previous spelling test score each week. It wasn't my most creative idea, but it was all I had so I rolled with it. My students weren't huge fans of the mandated weekly spelling tests, and neither was I, but the bell made it at least a little more exciting. After grading the spelling tests over the weekend and returning them on Monday morning along with their new list, my students would get to take turns ringing the bell if they tied or improved their score from the previous week. My students took it upon themselves to give a roaring round of applause each time the bell was rung, and the student who was ringing the bell would bow or curtsy to show their appreciation for their classmates' support. Spelling test scores were skyrocketing and my students were growing closer, all thanks to a little gold bell.

That year, February 17 was a Monday, but since Valentine's Day had fallen on the Friday before, I gave my students a week off from their spelling test. Since I had no graded tests to return, I used the time to discuss National Random Acts of Kindness Day, which happened to fall on that day. I explained to my second graders what a random act of kindness was, gave examples, and encouraged them to participate throughout the day.

My students all nodded their heads in agreement, but one student raised her hand and asked, "Since we don't get to ring the bell for our spelling tests today, how about we ring the bell when we notice someone doing a random act of kindness instead?" A smile slowly spread across my face from ear to ear. Her idea was genius.

The bell was rung so many times that day that our hands were red and sore from clapping, but it was worth it. We resumed our typical bell ringing for spelling test scores the following Monday, but the tradition of also ringing the bell to acknowledge acts of kindness was born. My students never had to ask permission to ring the bell. They would just walk up to my desk, ring the bell, call out the act of kindness, and the class would clap.

I know this would drive some teachers crazy, but for me, the few seconds of noise and distraction were always worth the excitement it brought my students.

ENGAGEMENT DOESN'T HAVE TO BE FANCY

Even the most enthusiastic teachers will encounter aspects of teaching that just aren't exciting. There will be topics and skills you have to teach that are dull and boring. There will be assessments you have to administer that you and your students dread. There will be curriculums you have to follow that aren't engaging for your students. But if you aren't excited to teach a lesson, you can't expect students to be excited to learn it.

When I was entering second grade as a student, school wasn't exactly my favorite place to be. I had figured out in first grade that I was placed in one of the lowest reading groups, because the books we read were clearly much thinner, had more pictures, and contained fewer words in comparison to the other groups. My confidence with learning was at an all-time low, until I met my second grade teacher, Mr. Pelan.

Our classroom was located in a small portable outside of the main building, so space was limited, but it still felt like walking into Disney World every morning. I had never been to Disney World at the time, but our classroom was exactly how I imagined it looking. The entire back wall of the portable was covered in an array of hanging hats from princess headdresses to pirate tricorns that were incorporated into lessons and worn by students as an earned reward. Mr. Pelan had a bin of puppets, each with a unique voice, and he played his acoustic guitar in class every day. At the end of the school year, he gave each student a cassette tape (if that doesn't scream 1990s, I'm not sure what does) with recordings of all the songs he wrote and sang to us throughout the year. I still have mine to this day.

Mr. Pelan was by far the most engaging teacher I have ever had, and his enthusiasm for teaching completely changed my attitude toward learning. I went from hating school to loving it, and would rise from the lowest reading group to a straight-A student through college. All it took was a few hats, some puppets, an acoustic guitar, and a passion for exciting students.

When students are engaged in a lesson, their focus increases, unwanted behavior problems decrease, and long-term retention of the knowledge strengthens. But in the world of teaching, "engaging" is often synonymous with "over the top." Many teachers mistakenly believe they have to deck out their classroom from floor to ceiling with themed decorations and materials to get their students' attention. They think they have to choreograph an entire dance number to get students interested and spend hours planning extensive lessons to make learning fun. Student engagement doesn't have to be that fancy, and the planning behind it shouldn't be that hard.

At the surface level, Mr. Pelan's engagement strategies may sound ornate. I mean, recording a cassette tape of songs is pretty darn close to choreographing an entire dance number. But these "over-the-top" actions are all relative. Mr. Pelan was a musician in addition to being a teacher, which means writing songs, playing guitar, and recording music was in his wheelhouse. It didn't require learning a new skill, devoting copious amounts of time, or spending tons of money. Instead, he was able to utilize the strengths he already had as a person outside of the classroom to engage his students, myself included.

True engagement derives from connection. Students have to experience a desire to know more, understand why it matters, and feel empowered in their own learning to form a connection to the content. As the teacher, it is your job to capture student attention, make the learning relevant, and promote participation, which sounds daunting, especially in a world filled with instant gratification and constant distractions. But engagement can be achieved through small but meaningful adjustments to what you're already doing that complement your unique personality and teaching style.

SECURE THE INVESTMENT

The first step is to get your students to buy into the lesson. To put it another way, you have to give them a reason to care about what you are teaching. Think about a couple at a sporting event, where one person is a lifelong fan of the team playing and the other person could care less who wins. The former will cheer at the top of their lungs during every single play while the latter probably will scroll on their phone and is completely uninterested. When it comes to your teaching, you want your students to be die-hard fans of your lessons.

Some students may enter your classroom already wearing foam fingers, ready to cheer you on no matter what, but other students will feel like they're being dragged to a game they didn't want to attend in the first place. Either way, you have the power to increase your students' investment in your lessons.

You can start by invoking their curiosity. You want to have them questioning, wondering, and eagerly awaiting more information. This can be as simple as covering something in your room with butcher paper, putting a sealed box in the front of your room, or wearing a different outfit so your students are left guessing why.

Then, you need to find ways to make the lesson relevant to them. You have to establish why they should care and incorporate their interests along the way to keep their attention (this is why many sporting events have cheerleaders). Give your lessons a purpose by having students produce artifacts or information that will be shared with others, like creating posters that will be hung around the school, writing letters that will be mailed, or producing videos that will be sent to families, and include real-world examples they can relate to. If you're teaching a math lesson on angles and the number of degrees in a circle, you could show a quick video clip of a famous skateboarder performing a 360 trick to help make the connection. Relevancy can be established by including quick stories, visual examples, and materials related to things they care about.

Finally, you want to give students a choice. No one enjoys feeling forced to do something, and students are no exception. Offering a simple choice between two things is an easy way to switch the feeling from coerced to empowered. Give students opportunities to choose the activity they complete, the color paper they use, or the specific questions on a page they answer. If you want students to complete five practice problems, include ten on the page and let them choose which ones they want to solve.

These adjustments are simple and don't add a substantial amount of time to your lesson planning process, but they can drastically improve the level of student engagement.

ADD ENHANCEMENTS

Once your students are invested in a lesson, you have to sustain their interest. This is where enhancements come in. By adding basic props, music, and movement to your lessons, you can completely elevate the learning experience for students with minimal effort. I bet that the attendance at sporting events would significantly decrease if all the flashy lighting, upbeat music, and quirky memorabilia sold at the gift shop suddenly disappeared. Some fans may still show up to support their team (and grab a hotdog from the concession stand), but the overall excitement wouldn't be the same.

I am a firm believer that props make everything more fun. My mom was a dental hygienist and would volunteer to do a demo lesson on teeth brushing with my class every year when I was in elementary school. She would show up to the classroom with a bag packed full of props including models of your jaw and teeth she had collected during her training and different sized toothbrushes. It was a little embarrassing at the time, but the other students in my class always *loved* it. Finding simple ways to add physical props to your lesson can almost instantly pique student interest. Here are a few of my personal favorites:

- **Food.** After checking with families to confirm student allergies, incorporate food items into your lessons. I had students use candy corn as math manipulatives in October (and jellybeans in the spring), create three-dimensional models of shapes using mini marshmallows and toothpicks, and use chocolate chip cookies to model fossil excavation.

- **Clothes.** Think about how your outfit choice can make an experience feel more real and exciting for students. I wore a rainbow lab coat during science experiments, put on an oversized pair of novelty glasses when we needed to take a "closer look" at a text, and dressed up as an old lady to celebrate the one hundredth day of school (complete with mints in my purse to give out).

- **Plastic tablecloths.** These are cheap, colorful, and can be used for *so* many things! I covered my students' desks in blue tablecloths when we started our ocean unit, white tablecloths when my students became doctors during "text feature surgery" (details on that below), and even draped tablecloths over chairs to create tents for my students to read under.

- **Quiet spray.** I taped a label on an empty spray bottle and convinced my students it was filled with a mysterious gas that would make my classroom go silent. They believed me and it worked wonders when I needed a quiet moment throughout the day.

- **Brain sprinkles.** I filled a sugar shaker from the dollar store with glitter and gave it a few shakes over top of my students' heads, with permission, or on their papers before assessments.

- **Trashketball.** Before assessments, I gathered review questions and placed my students on different teams to answer them collaboratively. Each time a team answered a question correctly, they got to shoot a ball into a trashcan to earn a bonus point. You can make it fancy by using mini basketballs and a trashcan shaped like a net or you can simply use a balled up piece of paper and the trashcan you already have in your classroom.

- **Text feature surgery.** My students performed "surgery" on various magazines and printed articles by identifying and removing the different text features. I gave my students surgical masks and gloves I found at the dollar store and they would attach the text features to their paper using bandages. Their desks were transformed into operating tables by adding a simple white tablecloth and I played heartbeat sounds through my computer while my students tended to their "patients."

Speaking of heartbeat sounds, music and sound effects are another easy way to enhance a lesson with minimal added effort. You can play instrumental music while students work (which is less distracting than music with lyrics), use sounds to get students' attention (a wireless doorbell is a great option for this and comes with tons of sound choices), play themed music when starting a new unit (think *Jurassic Park* before your paleontology unit), and use sounds to set a mood (play creepy music while students write scary stories).

Movement is essential in a classroom. If you get antsy sitting through an hour-long meeting, imagine how your students feel sitting at their desks for an entire school day. Provide your students with opportunities to move by incorporating brain breaks, transitions, and games in your instruction. Here are a few ideas you can use:

■ **Responses.** Pick a movement that corresponds with the answers to multiple-choice or true/false questions. For example, if you're reviewing the animal adaptations for a science unit, you can have students mimic an alligator mouth to answer A, flap their arms like a bat to answer B, crawl like a crab to answer C, and waddle like a duck to answer D.

■ **Class cheers.** Let students pick a cheer for the class to perform for them at various points of a lesson. You can encourage your students to create their own cheers that include movements and sound effects.

■ **Rock, paper, scissors.** Have students work as partners and play rock, paper, scissors to decide who has to answer the next question. Another option is to play rock, paper, scissors when you call on students during lessons. If the teacher wins, the student has to answer the question but if the student wins, the question gets passed to another student in the class.

■ **Sink or swim.** This is a review game you can play with students without any materials. Have all students stand up, split your class into two teams, and alternate asking each team a question. If a student on the team answers a question correctly, the team gets to choose between "sink" (they make a member of the other team sit down and be out of the game) or "swim" (they can make a member of their own team who is currently out come back into the game). You can add extra movement by having students walk over and quietly tap the student they want to "sink" on the shoulder. If a student on the team answers a question incorrectly, that student gets "sunk" and must sit down until they are brought back into the game.

■ **Snowball fights.** Write questions or problems on pieces of paper and crumble them up to create paper "snowballs." Allow students to have a "snowball fight" by tossing these balls around the room for a set period of time before picking one up and answering the question written on it. You can extend this activity by having students use a different strategy or add a new example each time the snowball is thrown and picked up, so the same papers can be used multiple times.

■ **Hot potato.** Play a quick game of hot potato after asking a question. Choose an item and play music while students pass it around (this is an opportunity for students to think about the answer to the question). When you stop the music, the student who is holding the item has to answer the question.

■ **Charades.** Give students opportunities to play charades when reviewing vocabulary by taking turns acting out certain words or phrases related to the content. Demonstrate for students how they can model the definitions through their movements. This can be done as a whole group activity or with small groups of students.

Together, these enhancements can help take your lesson to the next level without going over the top.

MAKE IT NOVEL

Even when your students are fully invested and you're sustaining their interest, you might still find the overall excitement in your classroom fading over time. Just like how a sports team releases new apparel or welcomes new players to keep fans energized, you want to do something new, fresh, and unique to add excitement when you or your students feel stuck in a routine.

Here are a few ways you can change up things in your classroom without extending your planning time or spending hundreds of dollars:

- Stand on a table or chair in the middle of a lesson.

- Teach from the back of the classroom instead of the front.

- Have your students sit backward in their chairs or on top of their desks (carefully, of course).

- Allow your students to write on their desks using dry erase markers (test this first to make sure it erases).

- Let students write with a colored pencil, pen, or marker for the day.

- Have students write in "invisible ink" (you can use real invisible ink pens or have them write with a white crayon and then color over it with a marker to reveal the writing).

- Take students outside (give them chalk to solve math problems or collect data for a science lab).

- Change your voice when reading.

- Turn off the lights and read by flashlight.

- Create an interpretive dance while reading an informational text (the worse you are at dancing, the more memorable it is for your students).

Not every lesson will be knocked out of the park. There will be days when teaching feels like you're going into overtime for a tied 0-0 game and half the crowd has already departed the stadium, leaving behind nothing but sticky seats and an assortment of crumbs on the floor. In these moments, you have to call an audible and change strategy. Having a bag full of tricks ready to engage your students makes it much easier to win back the fans and have the crowd's support for the next homerun.

YOUR HOMEWORK

Put together a list of engagement ideas. This is the "bag of tricks" you can get ideas from any time you can feel the excitement in your classroom dwindling. Keep the list in your lesson planner or in a note-taking app on your phone for easy reference when you need inspiration and only add the ideas that align with your teaching style or you are excited to try.

Plan a lesson around the latest student craze. Trends are constantly changing but find what your students are obsessed with currently and incorporate it into a lesson. It could be a new video game, a new toy, or a new TV show or movie. If you aren't sure what the latest craze is, just ask your students. They will be happy to tell you all about it. After checking online to make sure the trend is appropriate, collaborate with your team teachers to plan a lesson around it that your students will be excited to learn.

Build anticipation for an upcoming unit or lesson. Look at your calendar for the next month and choose an upcoming unit or lesson you know you'll be teaching. It's best if this is a unit or lesson you aren't looking forward to teaching because you know it's challenging for students or the content simply isn't engaging. Take time to consider how you can pique interest and get students guessing what they will be learning before you even start the unit or lesson.

Commit to enhancing a lesson you're teaching in the next week. Think about how you can add props, music, or movement to make the lesson more engaging for students. Remember, this should be *easy* and not require a lot of extra time, work, or money to implement. You can brainstorm ideas while you're driving to or from school, taking a shower, or waiting for dinner to heat up in the microwave.

Incorporate something novel within the next week. Find a way to change things up in your classroom or during a lesson in the next week. Make one simple change that your students aren't expecting to add excitement.

Remember, student engagement doesn't have to be a big dog-and-pony show with performances daily at 8:00 a.m. sharp. The best tool you have to capture student attention, ignite their desire to know more, and sustain their interest in the lesson is yourself. There is no other teacher and there will never be another teacher exactly like you. Your personality, unique quirks, and individual strengths are the most powerful way to connect with your students and make them care about what you are teaching.

As you develop and embrace your own personal teaching style, it can be tempting to compare it with those around you, or even those you see online but don't know personally. It's vital to your happiness and confidence as a teacher that you avoid this slippery slope and remain true to yourself, but that's obviously easier said than done.

CHAPTER 8

A Classroom Isn't Always Cleaner on the Other Side

The longer you teach, the more likely you are to become known for something. Among your students, you may be known for wearing wacky outfits, singing songs in class, or teaching a fun and engaging lesson every year. I once had a high school teacher who was known for wearing a different tie every single day of the school year. Every morning, you would find students peeking their heads through his classroom doorway to check what his tie was for the day. They may have had the typical "I'm too cool for school" teenage attitude, but they still had to know what tie he was wearing. Among your coworkers, you may be known for always having a desk drawer stocked with candy and snacks (this is a great way to make new friends, by the way), a cabinet full of craft supplies, or having the magical touch that could always fix the copy machine.

I once worked with a teacher who was known for always arriving at school on time and leaving school on time. If teachers had to report to school at 8:00 a.m., this teacher was strolling up to the entry doors at 7:59 a.m. If our contracted hours ended at 4:00 p.m., she was out the door and halfway to her car by 4:01 p.m.

I always watched her come and go from the building with awe. The only items in her hand were her purse, car keys, and a lunch box. She seldom took any work home and yet her papers were always graded and her lessons were always flawless. It truly seemed effortless for her, like she had it down to a science.

She was my idea of "teacher goals." She had somehow established balance between her work life and personal life, which always felt so far out of reach in my world. I would look at her and wonder, "How the heck does she do it all and how long is it going to take me to get to that point?!" I admired her, but I also was envious of her.

I worked so hard and so long to get everything done and still wasn't successful. I got to school an hour early every morning to make last-minute copies, organize my materials for the day, and try to squeeze in some grading before the bell rang. I stayed at school several hours each night to straighten student desks, put materials away, attempt to lesson plan, and continue creating the classroom of my dreams. No matter how efficient I was with my time, there were still never enough hours in the day to get it all done. Yet, I looked at her and was reminded that it apparently was possible because she was doing it. That inner voice in my head started whispering, "You're not good enough," and I started listening to it.

But, my efforts helped me become known for two things among my coworkers. First, I became known for notoriously being the last car to leave the parking lot each night. In fact, my coworkers often called or texted me late at night to turn off lights they left on in their classroom or retrieve a lunch box they left because they knew I would still be there. I wore it like a badge of honor, but in hindsight, this wasn't a good thing to become known for. The long hours were unsustainable, which eventually led to burnout. But, we'll come back to that because that topic deserves its own spotlight.

The second thing I became known for was my immaculate classroom organization. I had plastic bins with matching labels for every single item stored in my cabinets. I had organizers lining every drawer, color-coded binder clips for every subject, and neatly assembled binders for every unit. I'm a little bit biased, but it was a thing of beauty.

My husband did have to establish a "bin ban" at one point because my bin purchasing habit was a little out of control, but that's a story for another day.

One Friday after school, I was sitting at my classroom desk trying to finalize my lesson plans for Monday. Friday afternoons were some of my most productive work hours because the teachers at my school always rushed out as soon as the students were dismissed. I could blast some music, use the copier uninterrupted, and get all the things done I hadn't been able to accomplish earlier in the week. I was belting out the chorus of Journey's "Don't Stop Believin'" when I heard a knock on my door.

"Hey, do you have a second?"

It was the teacher who was known for always leaving school on time. Poking her head through my door. At 4:15 p.m.

"Yeah . . . yeah, of course. What's up?" I struggled to formulate a response because I was in shock that she was still at school. I was worried something was seriously wrong because this never happened. Ever.

"I was wondering if you'd be able to help me set up some kind of organization system for all my cabinets. I've been neglecting them and it's gotten a little out of control. I've been a little jealous of how neat yours are."

It turns out, the teacher who I had been envious of for her work-life balance was envious of my organized classroom. All those times I looked at her and wished I could be more like the teacher she was, she was looking at me and wishing her classroom could be more like mine. The tables were turned and I realized that none of us actually have it all together, despite how it may seem from the outside.

COMPARISON IS A LIE

Even the most organized teacher has a disorganized, hot mess of a junk drawer hiding somewhere in their classroom. It's probably in the back corner of the room and tucked behind a chair, but it's there. As teachers and as people, we all have our own messes, but some of us are better at hiding them than others.

Sometimes it feels like our own messes are illuminated under a spotlight. Since we know exactly where they are, either physically or metaphorically, we assume everyone else is aware of them, too. But when we look around at others, we never see their messes. We only see the most put together aspects of their lives, because that's what they choose to show us (and I don't blame them). But this spotlight effect on our own shortcomings paired with the shadow effect on everyone else's leaves us feeling inferior.

We've all done it. We've all become jealous of another classroom that appears cleaner, more organized, or more aesthetically pleasing than ours. We've all been attacked by the green-eyed monster when a student tells us they like another teacher more because they're funnier, trendier, cooler, or easier. We've all played it off like we don't care that our classroom isn't picture perfect or that the comment didn't bother us, but deep down, we're hurt.

Comparison is a natural human tendency. So many aspects of our society are hierarchical and this ranking system becomes ingrained in our mind. But although it's natural, comparison isn't realistic or helpful.

When we make a comparison, we're forming opinions using surface-level information. We can only see what's happening on the outside and our eyes are shielded from what's happening underneath. When you see another teacher leaving school on time every day, it's easy to think, "Must be nice! I wish I didn't have to stay late." But in reality, that teacher actually spends all weekend working. When you see another teacher with a beautiful classroom, you may feel envious of the space they've created but don't realize they spent thousands of dollars out of their own pocket to bring it to life. You see the results but not the efforts. The highlight reel you're watching doesn't show you all the behind-the-scenes work, time, energy, or money that went into creating it.

Our comparisons also tend to be unfair. We compare apples to oranges and rank them based on a few select criteria, without considering the unique differences both have to offer. When we compare the strengths of others with weaknesses of our own, the results are rigged. It's like giving someone else a head start in a race and then feeling upset when you lose when you didn't give yourself a fair chance to begin with. New teachers compare themselves with veteran teachers, teachers with families compare themselves with single teachers, and older teachers compare themselves with younger teachers. It's impossible to fairly compare two things that aren't on a level playing field to begin with.

Playing these comparison games is a waste of your valuable time and energy as a teacher. There's no winner, but you're awarded with lower self-esteem, feelings of inferiority, anxiety, jealousy, and resentment as your consolation prize just for playing. Rather than moving you forward on your own journey, they distract you and shift your focus to things outside of your control. You can never change what other people do, but you are in control of your own actions and beliefs and can take steps to avoid this game altogether.

FIND THE TRUTH

Avoiding the comparison game begins with finding the truth behind comparison myths. These are the little things we tell ourselves or choose to believe during a bout of comparison that simply aren't accurate but fuel our feelings of inferiority.

The first one is a standard of perfection. When we believe the myth that perfection exists and is attainable, we continuously work toward achieving it. Our brains become wired to automatically search for strengths in others and weaknesses in ourselves as an attempt to move closer to the end goal. We observe a high level of student engagement during another teacher's lesson and become more aware that ours is lacking. We watch another teacher interacting positively with a student's parent after school and realize our family connections need strengthening. We notice the quick and efficient transitions between activities in another classroom and recognize that ours need improvement.

But as much as we may strive for it, perfection is an illusion. Real life isn't social media where every piece of content shared has been filtered to hide imperfections, every feed has been curated to establish a desired aesthetic, and every picture has been edited to look flawless. In the real world, perfection is an unattainable and unrealistic goal to set for ourselves, but yet it still becomes a standard against which we measure our abilities. Our desire for perfection blurs the way we look at ourselves and others. It causes our minds to highlight the strengths we see in others, since those appear closer to the goalpost of perfection, and pit them against the weaknesses we see in ourselves, since those are seemingly holding us back.

We have to combat this myth by accepting imperfection. When we recognize that flaws are to be expected and weaknesses are unavoidable, we can set a more attainable goalpost to work toward. We can shift our focus to our strengths, which were previously hidden in the shadows of our weaknesses, and create a plan to improve our shortcomings, but not to the standard of perfection. We can accept that we will always be growing as teachers and trying to improve. We can appreciate that every teacher is unique and has different strengths. We can be grateful for the opportunity to learn from the experience, knowledge, and talents of others. The comparison game flips from external to internal, which allows us to prioritize our own progress over the achievement of an unrealistic goal.

Another myth we find ourselves believing is that external signs of success are equated with happiness. We look for the things we desire in others, like an organized classroom, a favorable evaluation, or a frivolous award, and assume anyone who has those things must be happy. We tell ourselves our unhappiness stems from what we have yet to achieve, and use the achievements of others to set a new standard for our own success. We believe we will be happy once we have those same material measures of success, but continuously move the goalpost further and further away. Once we achieve what we originally desired but still haven't found happiness, we convince ourselves we need more.

But happiness is not always in line with outward representations of achievement. Just because someone else appears to have the things you desire doesn't mean they are happy or better, and just because you achieve the things you desire doesn't mean you will be either. When you separate your feeling of worth from your level of achievement, you build organic happiness from present experiences instead of relying on future goals. Equating your value as a teacher with your intentions and impact allows you to stop using comparisons as a measure of your worth. You will find more happiness through the desires you have for your students, the joy you bring to their lives, and the growth you help them make than a "Teacher of the Year" award could ever bring you.

We also assume the myth of a ranking system. We place every idea, action, person, and achievement into an imaginary hierarchy to determine superiority. We make comparisons to figure out which is better, and use that as the desired standard. We compare classrooms, teaching styles, lesson ideas, grading systems, and approaches to classroom management using this ranking system and feel inferior if ours falls short on the hierarchy. As the pressure to move up in the rankings builds, we sacrifice our authenticity. We mimic what we see other teachers doing because we believe it scores higher on the imaginary scale and, therefore, must be better, which causes us to lose sight of our own unique qualities and strengths as teachers.

The truth is everything in life isn't organized on a ranking system. Sometimes one way isn't necessarily better than another way. It's just different. Two teachers can have drastically different approaches to classroom management and one doesn't have to be better than the other. They can both be effective and they can both hold value. When you let go of the pressure to do what you see teachers doing, you gain confidence in your own approach. You realize that what works for them may not work for you, and that's okay. Your classroom doesn't have to operate within the same set of rules as another and your teaching style doesn't have to mirror anyone else's.

When you learn to challenge these comparison myths, you stop looking to others for affirmation and turn to the only person who can truly validate your worth, and that is yourself.

KEEP YOUR EYES ON YOUR OWN PAPER

This process starts with accepting where you are currently. Everyone is in a different season of life that comes with its own unique challenges, yourself included. Despite the fact that you aren't a perfect teacher, you may not be as far along in your journey as others, and you're making mistakes along the way, you are doing the best you can. Give yourself grace. Just like every PhD graduate was once a kindergarten student who didn't know how to read, every veteran teacher was once a brand new teacher who didn't know how to write an effective lesson plan, anticipate student struggles along the way, or differentiate to meet a diverse range of needs. We all have to start somewhere.

Whether a student enters kindergarten already knowing how to read or unable to recite the alphabet yet, there is still room for growth. As a teacher, your progression is more important than your starting point. Rather than using other teachers as a standard for comparison, you have to keep your eyes on your own paper and strive for improvement. Your goal is always to become a better version of yourself, not to mirror someone else's journey.

But when the path of improvement is rocky, your progress feels slow, and the finish line is nowhere in sight, it's easy to lose motivation. You have to celebrate the small victories you experience along the way to fuel your journey and regain momentum. If you get observed and your evaluation is slightly higher than before, pat yourself on the back. If you finally connect with a student who has been withdrawn, commemorate it. If you have all of your lessons for the next week planned before you leave school on Friday for the first time all year, take time to treat yourself. You're allowed to celebrate tiny steps in the right direction even if you haven't reached your final destination yet. A victory doesn't have to be massive to deserve praise. The more small celebrations you include in your journey, the more confident you become that you will achieve your end goal and the more likely you are to reach the finish line.

Every time you look at another teacher and see a quality you desire, there is another teacher looking at you and thinking the same thing. You are someone else's goals. You are someone else's idea of the teacher they want to be. You are someone else's inspiration.

TURN COMPARISON INTO INSPIRATION

When comparison results in envy, that is a sign the other person has something you desire. If you get jealous when another teacher is offered the position of team lead, that shows you want to be seen by your peers or superiors as a leader. Rather than resenting what the other person has, channel the energy into action so you can get it for yourself. Develop your leadership skills such as communication, creativity, and problem-solving to increase your chances of being offered a similar position in the future. Turn your source of comparison into inspiration to become a better version of yourself instead of letting it discourage your efforts.

When the secretary informed me over the intercom that students were being moved to other classes during my first year, I had a choice to make. I could let it defeat me as a teacher before my year had even started, or I could use it to light a fire under my new teacher butt and prove to the world (or at least my school community) I could be an effective teacher. You already know which one I picked. Instead of comparing myself to the other teachers in my grade and feeling shame in my lack of experience, I used the situation as a springboard to launch my progress forward. I found my inspiration.

I couldn't change the current situation, but I could create the one I wanted for the future. I knew I could only get better as I gained more experience and I was determined to end the school year as a much stronger teacher than when I started it. Instead of calling to request their child be moved out of my class, I wanted families calling to request their child be put into my class. It wouldn't be easy, but I was willing to put in the work it would take to make that happen. And it did.

Comparison can either blur the way you view yourself and others or it can create a clear image of what you want, depending on how you use it. It can be a hindrance that holds you back or a boost that moves you forward. Replace comparison with collaboration and use the teaching community as inspiration to grow, develop, and improve your abilities as an educator. When teachers join forces, embrace their differences, and advance together, the entire field of education benefits.

YOUR HOMEWORK

Adopt a mantra. Find a simple phrase you can repeat to yourself in moments when you catch yourself playing the comparison game. Here are a few examples:

- You do you.
- The grass isn't always greener.
- I am on my own journey.
- Keep your head down and your eyes forward.
- Stay in your own lane.
- Nobody is perfect.
- Some people hide their messes better than others.
- The success of others does not limit my own.
- Envy shows me what I want but it's up to me to get it.
- Comparison is a distraction to my own journey.

Practice gratitude. This helps highlight your achievements, bring attention to your growth, and assigns value to what you already have. Make it a habit to write down at least one thing you're grateful for every day in a journal, your lesson planner, or a notebook. This daily practice becomes a record you can look back on when you are feeling inadequate or negative.

Detox your social media. Take note of how you feel when you spend time browsing social media. Unfollow people who trigger comparisons or make you feel worse about yourself. Follow new accounts that inspire you or help remind you of your strengths. Delete the apps for a scheduled period of time and consider asking a friend to be your accountability buddy during the process if you need extra support.

Create a hype playlist. Add songs to your playlist that make you feel good about yourself, remind you of pleasant memories, and hype you up. Listen to the playlist when you find yourself thinking negatively about yourself and your abilities.

Set an exciting goal. Instead of focusing on your shortcomings, start working toward a goal to help you improve in an area of choice. If you're jealous of another teacher who is always planned two weeks ahead, set a goal to have the following week's lesson plans ready by Friday and plan something exciting to do over the weekend to celebrate. Here is a list of other goals you could set:

- Earn a new degree or certification.
- Complete a training or online course.
- Learn a new skill or take up a new hobby.
- Work toward a promotion or apply for a new position.
- Foster a new friendship.
- Prioritize your self-care.
- Read more books.

- Leave school by a set time or limit the hours you will work outside of school.
- Join a new club or attend a meetup.
- Build a new habit or follow a new routine.

I wish I could promise you that the comparison game you will find yourself playing against other teachers eventually goes away, but in my experience, it doesn't. When your desire is to be the best teacher possible for your students, you can't help but evaluate your abilities and using the characteristics of others as a guide is an easy way to do that. But in those moments when you feel inferior, you have to remind yourself that perfection isn't reality, not everything exists on a ranking system, and your happiness should not depend on outward representations of success.

You are on our own journey and that journey is going to be filled with highs and lows just like everyone else's. As a teacher, you're going to experience shortcomings, make wrong choices, and receive criticism. But learning how to enjoy the journey despite these challenges is what makes arriving at the destination so rewarding. The best teachers aren't born, they're made. They're molded through their experiences and shaped through their growth, so every challenge is an opportunity to move closer to the desired outcome.

CHAPTER 9

Don't Get Your Stickers in a Twist

Getting observed as a teacher is a lot like competing in the Olympics. The athletes spend years devoting their lives to a sport, dedicate countless hours to training every week, and make numerous sacrifices to achieve a desired level of greatness, only to have their abilities judged by a single performance. One failed attempt seemingly can erase years of hard work in a matter of seconds and you can't help but think to yourself, "No! Wait! Let them try one more time! I'm sure they can do it if you just give them another chance!"

As a teacher, you spend years developing your craft, dedicating countless hours to the profession every week, and making numerous sacrifices to give your students the education they deserve. Your abilities are then evaluated during a single lesson, and sometimes, not even the whole lesson. It doesn't matter that your students understood the lesson you taught yesterday if they don't understand the lesson you're teaching during this small window of time being observed, critiqued, and ultimately used to determine your effectiveness as a teacher.

There are no "Teacher Olympics" (although I can confirm that teaching does sometimes feel as exhausting as running a marathon) and there may not be a podium to stand on, but you can still experience the feeling of a gold medal slipping out of your fingers from a single negative observation. You can feel your heart shatter in a million pieces as the result of a thirty-minute visit from a stranger stepping foot inside your classroom for the first time and judging your abilities as a teacher.

I faced my first extremely negative evaluation during a surprise observation in my third year of teaching. It wasn't career-ending or anything like that, but it was devastating enough to make me question my value and worth as a teacher. My observation had been conducted by a specialist in the county who I had never met until that day. Her arrival was unannounced and happened to coincide with my lunch time, so I had to forgo eating to answer her questions prior to starting the observation. I was a bundle of nerves (and my stomach was probably growling), but I brought my students back from the cafeteria and proceeded to teach the small group reading lesson I had planned. It wasn't a show-stopping lesson by any means, but it was typical. I felt like my students were engaged, understood the content being taught, and were able to demonstrate their learning. I was satisfied, especially under the circumstances.

A week later, I met with the same person who conducted my observation to review the results of my evaluation. The meeting ended with me in tears. I don't remember everything that was said, but I remember how I felt. Defeated. Inadequate. Worthless.

I spent the next few hours replaying the meeting in my head and what started as feelings of worthlessness and heartbreak quickly developed into anger and resentment. I had received negative feedback and criticism with prior observations, but this one felt different. This one felt personal.

That night, I ranted to Billy. I told him how unfair it was that I had to miss my lunch. I told him how wrong it was for someone to judge my teaching when they don't even know my students. I told him how ridiculous it was that I was being torn apart for such small things. He listened and nodded. I felt like he was getting it.

When I was finally done pacing around the room and letting out all my frustrations, he responded and said, "It sounds like you need a Q-tip."

My anger suddenly redirected from the evaluation to him.

"Why the heck would I need a Q-tip?! It sounds like you need one because your ears clearly aren't hearing what I'm saying!"

He laughed and clarified.

"Q-tip means 'quit taking it personally.' This evaluation isn't a reflection of you as a person. It isn't an attack. It's just feedback."

Those were the exact words I needed to hear at that moment. My anger didn't subside immediately, but it did cool off enough for me to think about the situation more objectively.

IT'S NOT YOU, IT'S THEM

You could have five different people observe the exact same lesson at the exact same time and you will get five completely different evaluations. Teaching is a science, but it is also an art. This means it is subjective, abstract, and emotional. You have to accept that not everyone will understand your vision, agree with your methods, or appreciate your style.

But like an artist, you have to develop thick skin and learn not to take things personally. The judgments, comments, and criticisms you receive as a teacher are more reflective of the perspective and opinion of the individual giving them than they are of your abilities and practices. To put it simply, it's not you, it's them.

Opinions will surround you as a teacher like dirt on the playground. You'll be exposed to feedback from superiors, unsolicited advice from coworkers, and haphazard critiques from families. It's easy to internalize these outside opinions, especially when they are negative. It's okay to use these beliefs as a catalyst for reflection, but when the opinions of others begin to distort and alter your opinion of yourself, the internalization has gone too far.

A difference of opinion can ignite your emotions like wildfire, especially when the opinion is related to something you are extremely passionate about, like teaching. But when you are emotionally charged, you are not your best self. Your reactions become raw and difficult to control and your judgment becomes clouded. You might get angry, become defensive, feel shameful, or shut down completely. This involuntary response can lead to saying or doing things you might not mean or might regret.

It isn't realistic to never take things personally, but that isn't an excuse to avoid developing a thick skin altogether. You still have to do some internal work to figure out why certain things bother you. You have to become mentally and emotionally strong enough to withstand the conflicting opinions of others without making them about you. You have to develop an unwavering confidence in your worth, value, and abilities both as a teacher and as a person.

FIND YOUR TRIGGERS

Grab a shovel because this is where the digging starts. To stop taking things personally, you have to first figure out the behind-the-scenes reason for why a comment or behavior feels like a personal attack.

When you first start to dig below the surface, you will find the experiences that shaped you. Our lives are all different and these differences result in unique perspectives, opinions, and beliefs that affect how we interpret the words and actions of others. Our experiences become the lens through which we view the world around us. It's like our own personal pair of glasses and only our eyes can see clearly through our prescription. We put these glasses on every day and perceive situations through our unique lens, which means we see everything just a little bit differently than the people around us.

But if you keep digging, eventually you will find a negative core belief hidden deep below the surface. This is a negative, internal opinion you hold about yourself that you believe to be true. It could be that you're not good enough, you're a failure, you're weak, you're unlovable, you're not important, or you're broken. This core belief forms as a result of your life experiences and often emerges as your internal dialogue, or the things you tell yourself. It's like a small scratch in your lens that makes it harder to see things clearly.

Chances are, the reason you're taking something personally is because it triggered your negative core belief.

Something that was said or done in a situation validated the negative voice inside your head that you're constantly trying to silence. The rude email from a parent reminded you that you really aren't good enough. The snarky comment from a student reminded you that you really are unlovable. The harsh criticism from an administrator reminded you that you really are a failure. An insecurity you may not have even known you had until that moment has been brought to the surface and with it comes a lot of emotions. Most of them are negative.

When this happens, you usually start ruminating. You replay the situation over and over again in your head like a movie. You overanalyze every single word and gesture and attach meaning to them. You continue to listen to that inner voice reminding you of your negative core belief, which causes it to become louder and louder. You find yourself repeating a never-ending cycle of thoughts and questions that don't lead you any closer to the answers you're looking for.

Rather than letting a trigger define you, you can use it to flip the switch on your negative core belief. Your triggers can be used as tools to help you discover the negative opinions you hold about yourself and opportunities to practice reversing the thoughts.

You can start by figuring out why a comment or behavior bothers you. What did the words or action mean to you? Did they remind you of another experience you've had? Did they elicit specific emotions? Did they trigger the voice inside your head? If so, what did the voice say? The answers to these questions will help guide you toward identifying the negative things you believe to be true about yourself.

Then, you can recognize when your negative core belief is causing you to ruminate and break the thought cycle by distracting yourself. For example, when you find yourself lying in bed at night repeating a critique you received from an administrator over and over again in your head, you can recognize this pattern of rumination and read a book or listen to a podcast to get your mind off of it. This will prevent the downward spiral and give you an opportunity to practice reversing the thoughts when you are in a clearer headspace, such as the next morning when you wake up. You can challenge every negative thought and replace it with a realistic one. If you find your inner voice saying, "I knew I was a horrible math teacher," you can flip the switch and tell yourself, "I can take action to improve."

Sometimes our personal lenses distort or alter how we interpret situations, which results in a warped perspective of reality. We internalize criticisms to be attacks on our character instead of considering how they could be reflective of someone else's experience. When you feel yourself taking something personally, slow down and find ways to see the situation more clearly.

CLEAN YOUR LENS

If you've ever played the game telephone, you know how quickly and easily messages can get distorted when they are passed from person to person. What started as "I love cheeseburgers" somehow gets twisted into "I left the cap off my markers" after just a few whispering passes from one person to the next. The unique lenses through which we see the world cause every interaction with others to play out like a game of telephone.

Every communication between you and another person has to pass through two different sets of lenses, the other persons' and your own, and the communication gets slightly distorted each time it passes through a lens. This distortion causes misinterpretations that then fog up our lenses and cloud our vision further.

You have to clean your lens as often as possible to see situations clearly.

One way you can clean your lens is by checking your ego. You have to give yourself tough love and consider if you are making a situation about you when it isn't. Did someone cut a conversation short and you wonder what you did to cause it? Did someone not respond to your text and you assume they don't like you? Did someone not save you a seat at the meeting and you think about why they're mad at you? Think about possible explanations for the action that don't involve you. Is the other person going through something so they didn't feel like talking? Did they lose their phone so they can't access their texts? Did they just forget you had asked them to save you a seat? Put yourself on the back burner and consider what could be happening below the surface that has nothing to do with you.

Your lens can also be cleaned through self-reflection. Every criticism you receive is an opportunity to check the prescription of your lens and determine if you need an adjustment. Being able to interpret critiques as feedback is a vital component of professional growth. Rather than receiving a constructive comment as insulting or offensive, reframe your perspective. Use it as a chance to identify underlying weaknesses and strengthen them before more damage is done. But, reflection doesn't have to be synonymous with acceptance. You can receive criticism, reflect on your own opinions, and ultimately come to a different conclusion. Your teaching style is unique to you, and should never be sacrificed to be seen clearly through someone else's lens.

Another way to clean your lens is by employing empathy. Your view through someone else's lens may always be blurry and unfocused since your life experiences haven't been the same, but try to adjust your eyes to a different perspective. Think about alternative interpretations of a situation beyond your own. If you struggle to put yourself in someone else's shoes (or see through someone else's lens), consider sharing the situation with a trusted friend or colleague who may be able to offer new perspectives you hadn't been able to see on your own. If you're interpreting an email from a parent as insulting and rude, try reading the email to a coworker (without sharing the parent's or student's name) to see how else it could be interpreted through a different lens. Considering how someone else's life story has shaped their lens allows you to better understand their perspective and avoid judging it for being different than yours.

When you take the time to check your lens for obstructions that could potentially warp your perspective, you gain a more transparent view of the situation.

STOP REACTING AND START RESPONDING

Once your lens is crystal clear, you can respond appropriately instead of reacting impulsively.

A proper response starts with restraint. You have to train yourself not to immediately reply to an email, speak up in a conversation, or take action until you've had enough time to process the situation. When you become offended or take things personally, you tend to jump to conclusions that aren't there to confirm your biases and validate your feelings.

But words are just words and actions are just actions until we as people assign meaning to them. You have to develop restraint and avoid making assumptions about the intention behind the words and actions in a situation until you have more information. You are not a mind reader and can't know the true meaning behind the words or actions until you ask.

Then, you have to give yourself space from the situation in question. When an experience is fresh, our emotions are heightened and distort our interpretation of what happened. We need time to neutralize our emotions and think about the situation more clearly. During this time, we can figure out what information we are missing, how we can gather that information to interpret the situation more accurately, and develop a spectrum of responses that can be employed based on the feedback we get from our initial response.

The final step is to get clarification. Ask questions to gather the information you need, present your interpretation of the situation to be checked for accuracy, and flexibly change your thinking when presented with new ideas. This is your response.

If a student is refusing to complete work you've assigned, you might interpret the situation as a personal attack on your teaching. You might assume the student hates you or wants to make your job more difficult. You might be tempted to move their seat closer to your desk to make them stay on task, take away recess time as a punishment, or say something like, "Well, if you don't do it now then it's going to become homework!" as a threat to provoke compliance. These are all examples of reactions. These are impulsive words and actions delivered without proper analysis of the situation. Instead, delay your response until you can gather more information to determine why they aren't completing their work. Walk away from the student and set a timer for a few minutes so you can think about what you want to say or do before responding. Consider the questions you might ask the student to get more information or what your next step will be if the student becomes agitated or upset. Then, get the clarification you need by asking the questions and offering solutions to problems that arise.

Depending on the situation, the best response might be no response. Sometimes the significance of the situation doesn't match the effort it would take to gain clarification, and it's best to just let it go. As long as you can avoid making assumptions and internalizing them, you can choose not to respond.

The transition from delivering spontaneous reactions to formulating strategic responses requires deliberate action and plenty of practice. But when mastered, this skill can help you gain more clarity in situations and prevent them from being interpreted as a personal attack.

YOUR HOMEWORK

Revisit a recent situation where you took things personally. Take time to consider why it triggered you and try to determine a negative core belief you hold. Try to identify assumptions you made and meaning you assigned to words or actions that weren't truly there. Reflect on the situation and consider other points of view by widening your perspective.

Find ways to cope with your triggers. Practice flipping the switch on your negative core belief by recognizing it and reversing the thoughts. Try grounding techniques like breathing, being mindful, self-soothing, visualization, journaling, and meditating. Reach out to someone if you need additional support.

Delay responding until you process the situation. You might need to develop a routine for getting out of a situation before you react. This could include a simple response such as "We need to come back to this at a later time" and an easy next step like walking away. If you need to get out your thoughts, type an email, text message, or letter but don't send it (if you're going to type an email, leave the recipient section blank just in case). After your emotions have regulated, process the situation and determine if it needs to be addressed. Remember, some things are worth letting go but some are worth addressing.

Notice when you are ruminating and distract yourself. Ruminating is when you keep thinking about a situation and overanalyze it. This process tends to be continuous and can lead you down a negative spiral if you don't catch it. If you keep replaying a conversation you had, an email you read, or an encounter you experienced in your head, call yourself out on ruminating. Then, find ways to distract yourself and get your mind off the situation. Here are a few ideas you can try:

- Go for a walk.
- Listen to music, a podcast, or an audiobook.
- Call a friend.
- Read a book.
- Exercise.
- Meditate.
- Take a nap.
- Do something creative.
- Watch a TV show, documentary, or movie.
- Organize a cabinet or drawer.

Find a place to keep positive notes from students, families, and colleagues. Screenshot text messages and add them to an album on your phone. Create an email folder to save emails or print them out. Get a box to keep in your classroom or at home to store all the notes that make you smile or remind you of your greater purpose. In those moments when you feel defeated or inadequate, you can look through the box and remember how big of a difference you make in the lives of others.

At its root, teaching is a personal profession but that doesn't mean every aspect of the job should be taken personally. There will be some criticisms that are valid and deserve personal reflection but there will be plenty of others that require a Q-tip to clean them out of your mind. Ultimately, your response to the criticism will always be more important than the words or actions themselves.

Teaching can easily take over your thoughts, actions, and even your entire life if you allow it to consume you. An email from a parent can replay in your head for days. Comments from an administrator can cause you to rewrite your lesson plans. A compliment from a student can make you want to devote all your free time to becoming a better teacher. While there may be times when this consumption is welcomed, especially early in your career, it's vital that you consider what you're giving up to make that happen.

CHAPTER 10

You Can't Have Your Apple and Eat It Too

I've always been a sucker for an award. It doesn't have to be anything fancy or overly exciting . . . even just a basic printed certificate is enough to send my motivation skyrocketing. In fact, I still have all the certificates I was awarded throughout my years of schooling tucked neatly in plastic page protectors and stored inside a binder for proper preservation. My personal favorite to receive was always the "Perfect Attendance" award, which unironically happens to be the award I received most often. From the first time I was awarded one in elementary school, I was hooked, and my determination to never miss a day of school became fueled.

Fast-forward to my first year of teaching when the excess of germs I was exposed to at school had other plans. Within the first month of school, I found myself down for the count and had to take my first sick day. Although my award-loving heart was crushed (not that we actually got "Perfect Attendance" awards as teachers, but one could pretend), I knew it was in everyone's best interest for me to stay home so the germs wouldn't be spread any further. I wrote the most detailed sub plans I could, submitted my absence into the system, and tried to push the guilty feeling far enough out of my mind that I could actually rest and recover.

When I returned to school the next day, my students smothered me in hugs and convinced me that I should "never do that to them again." They told me the substitute was mean, made them do work (I don't think they understood I was the one that actually assigned the work), and they had the worst day ever (remember what I said about students exaggerating things?). I knew this wasn't the truth, but it still hit me hard. The overwhelming feeling of guilt was back, and this time it was even stronger than before.

In an effort to avoid taking time off, I found myself playing a little game that could be appropriately titled "It's Just Allergies." The rules for the game are pretty simple. Anytime you feel under the weather, you tell yourself you're not actually sick, convince everyone around you it's allergies, start pounding some vitamin C supplements, and cross your fingers you wake up feeling better tomorrow. I became a master of this game. In hindsight, it was incredibly selfish and wrong of me to not stay home when I was clearly ill. But at the time, it felt like I was doing the right thing, or at least the thing would be the least inconvenient for others. Trying to secure a substitute wasn't always easy and this often meant my class would get split up between my team teachers if I had to take a sick day. So, on top of feeling guilty for not showing up for my students, I now felt even more guilty for making my team teachers' lives harder than they already were. It was a double-edged sword.

My solution was to hoard my sick days unless absolutely necessary, which did wonders for masking my feelings of guilt, but the side effects of never taking time off were less than desirable. Thus began the pattern of refusing to take days off school, overworking myself and running both my immune system and mental health into the ground, finally taking a day off, feeling guilty again, and then repeating the cycle. I would use one or two sick days a year out of my allotted ten, and bank the remaining days, which would roll over from year to year. I figured it made more sense to save them just in case a time came when I *really* needed them. Plus, I knew I could always have the accrued leave time paid out if and when I ever changed states in the future and my sick days didn't transfer.

Or so I thought.

In the spring of my seventh year of teaching, my husband and I made the decision to move halfway across the country from Maryland to Texas, which meant I had to say goodbye to a school I loved and resign from the district I was teaching in. After submitting my paperwork with plenty of notice, I began thinking about some of the details that came with resigning including the process for cashing out my remaining sick days.

Most districts have an employee handbook with all the information regarding terms of employment, responsibilities, and benefits that all employees are expected to read and abide by. But let's be honest, most of us do not take time to read the handbook from cover to cover and only look closely at it when we need the answer to a question.

Reviewing the leave guidelines my district had in place revealed some devastating news. My thirty-three days of accrued leave time was not eligible for payout since I had not taught in the district for at least ten years. This meant I was losing nearly 250 hours of banked time with no compensation. This meant I was losing nearly 250 hours of banked time I could have spent taking care of myself physically, mentally, and emotionally. This meant I had made a huge mistake.

Yes, I made the mistake of not thoroughly reading the employee handbook, and I take full responsibility for that lapse of better judgment. But that's not the huge mistake I'm referring to. I made the huge mistake of sacrificing my personal health and happiness for my profession, and that's one choice I sincerely regret.

MORE ISN'T ALWAYS BETTER

Teacher guilt is *real*. Education is such a noble and self-sacrificing field that you can't help but feel remorseful any time you put yourself first. But if you give all your time, attention, and energy to teaching, there won't be any left for other aspects of your identity. You have to remember that you are a person first and a teacher second.

I get it. You want to be the best teacher possible. After all, your students deserve the best education you can give them. It feels like you have to get to school early and stay at school late to achieve that goal. It feels like you have to dedicate every night, weekend, and holiday break to the profession to keep up. It feels like teaching has to be your everything all of the time or else you just aren't doing enough.

But the truth is more isn't always better. Sometimes more is just more, and can cause more harm than good. Too much sun creates a desert, too much ice cream gives you a stomachache, and too much self-sacrifice leaves teachers feeling exhausted and burnt out.

You have to ditch the martyr mentality. You have to stop sacrificing your own needs to provide a service to your students,
their families, and your school. My principal used to always tell
us, "If you were hit by a truck today, your job would be posted
tomorrow." It's a harsh wakeup call, but it's true. Teaching can
be your biggest passion, but it shouldn't be your entire life.

The universe operates on a balance of give and take. Every
second of time you give to one aspect of your life is a second
of time you have to take from somewhere else. Every ounce
of effort you give in one area is effort you don't have to give
in another. The more you give to teaching, the more you take
from your family and friends. The more you give to teaching,
the more you take from your health. The more you give to
teaching, the more you take from your passions, hopes, and
dreams outside of education.

You can convince yourself you're happy letting teaching
consume your life, but once you realize you keep giving more
and it's still never enough, it hits you.

You begin to feel taken advantage of.

You begin to feel resentful and bitter.

You begin to feel burnt out.

I heard about teacher burnout in college, but it always
sounded like an obscure fantasy. Just like I believed I would
be the anomaly and thrive as a first-year teacher, I believed I
would be the anomaly and somehow be magically immune to
teacher burnout. I thought burnout only happened to those
who weren't passionate enough, didn't put enough heart into
the profession, and simply didn't care enough to keep trying.

But teacher burnout doesn't discriminate.

It doesn't care how many years you've been teaching or
how much passion you have. It doesn't care that you wanted
to be a teacher since you were a little kid. It doesn't care
how badly you want to make a difference in the lives of your

students. If what you're doing is unsustainable, burnout will eventually find you.

Over the years, the number of hats teachers are forced to wear has increased dramatically. Teachers are no longer just teachers. They're also counselors, mentors, coaches, managers, protectors, and so many other important roles in the lives of their students. But while education has adapted to societal shifts for decades, the most drastic changes have occurred in just the past few years. The onset of a worldwide pandemic in 2020 presented unmeasurable challenges within education and resulted in skyrocketing rates of teacher burnout due to added responsibilities that only made teaching more difficult and unsustainable.

So how do you make teaching sustainable, especially when the field of education is always changing and new demands are constantly being introduced?

You set boundaries. When teaching consumes so much of your life, the lines between the parts of your identity become blurry. Boundaries help solidify those lines. They make it clear which hat you're wearing, how much time and energy you have to give, and, most importantly, when you need to say no.

FIND THE COMMITMENT COST

In case you needed a reminder, "no" is a complete sentence and doesn't require an explanation.

Can you help run the math committee this year? No.

Can you send home all the work this student will miss during a family vacation at the end of the month? No.

Will you cover lunch duty this week? No.

It's as simple as that.

No.

It's simple, but it isn't easy. In fact, in most cases, the easiest answer is "yes." When you say "yes," you're usually making someone else happy. You're making their life easier, but at what expense?

Most of the time, what's easy in the moment comes with a big cost you have to pay back later on. Sometimes your "yes" costs so much that you're drowning in debt but it's too late to make a return and get your money back. You're stuck paying it back, plus interest.

You have to consider the cost of the commitment.

Every time you say yes to one thing, you are saying no to something else. Before you give an answer, you have to consider what you're giving up. It could be time, energy, experiences, memories, or your overall happiness.

Ask yourself: If I say yes, what am I saying no to?

If you say "yes" to decorating the gym for an after-school event, you may be saying "no" to cheering on your son or daughter at their big game.

If you say "yes" to coming in early to tutor students, you may be saying "no" to the morning workout you love.

If you say "yes" to coaching an after-school team, you may be saying "no" to eating dinner with your family.

An even more powerful way to consider this decision is to acknowledge what you're able to gain because every time you say no to one thing, you get to say yes to something else. Saying no helps you get back what you lost when you said yes, including time, energy, experiences, memories, and your overall happiness.

Ask yourself: If I say no, what do I get to say yes to?

If you say "no" to leading an additional committee, you may be saying "yes" to having more time to work in your classroom before students arrive.

If you say "no" to volunteering at the school movie night, you may be saying "yes" to an opportunity to have a date night and reconnect with your significant other.

If you say "no" to covering lunch duty, you may be saying "yes" to enjoying your lunch and chatting with your coworkers, which gives you enough energy to make it through the rest of the day.

The people who always say "yes" will be the people who are always asked first. Break the cycle and say "no." It isn't easy, but neither is being indebted by expensive commitments. Both are hard, but you get to choose your hard.

FIND YOUR NONNEGOTIABLES

Just like you can't say yes to everything, you can't say no to everything either. You probably already know what's coming next. That's right . . . there has to be a balance. So how do you establish that balance and know when to say yes and when to say no?

If you can't say no to everything, you have to make sure you're saying no to the right things. You have to establish nonnegotiables.

Your nonnegotiables are the boundaries you refuse to budge on. These are the imaginary lines in your life you refuse to let others cross, no matter what, because you know they are in place to maintain your personal well-being.

This is where you get to be selfish and put yourself first. Think about what is important to you in life and what makes you happy. And not "I'm doing well, how are you?" happy, but your-face-hurts-from-smiling-so-much-yet-you-can't-stop happy. Those are the things you have to form a boundary around and protect at all costs. Anything that tries to cross that boundary gets an automatic "no," and the decision becomes much easier.

As you consider your nonnegotiables and the boundaries that will protect them, try matching an action (what you will or will not do) with a "why" (your deeper reason behind the action). Here are a few examples:

- I will not answer emails or phone calls after the school day ends (because I need to be present with my significant other).

- I will only work contract hours (because I want to pursue other passions in my free time).

- I will leave school no later than four o'clock (because I need to prioritize my health by going to the gym).

- I will not spend more than $100 on my classroom (because I need to save money for a down payment on a house).

- I will not work on anything school related over the weekend (because I value the time I spend with my family and friends).

Since each nonnegotiable is rooted in something important to you, the boundaries you establish do not need to be limited to your work responsibilities. This same principle can be applied to your classroom rules, expectations, and routines. Here are a few examples:

- Students need to keep all four legs of their chair on the floor (because their safety is most important).

- Students will read a book of choice for at least fifteen minutes every day in my classroom (because I want to instill a love of reading).

- Students will not make noise when walking in the hallway (because it is important to be respectful of other classes learning).

When you have a clear understanding of what's most important to you, it becomes far easier to let go of the guilt, align your actions to your priorities, and advocate for your own needs.

SET UP GUARDRAILS

Notice I said it becomes easier, not easy. Especially if you are a people-pleaser and struggle with saying no, it will probably never be easy to maintain your boundaries. You will have to work hard to clearly communicate your boundaries with others, hold yourself accountable, and take action when it is being pushed or crossed. A lot of people will use these obstacles as excuses for never setting boundaries in the first place.

If a kid (or adult) isn't great at bowling, no one says, "Eh, it's probably best to not even try." They simply find ways to make it easier. They give the kid a lighter ball, set up a ramp to slide the ball down, and raise the bumpers on either side of the lane to prevent the ball from rolling into the gutters. With a little support, the gutter balls suddenly turn into strikes and the game of bowling doesn't seem so difficult.

Just like bumpers in a bowling lane, guardrails are steps you can take and habits you can build that make it easier to preserve your boundaries. Here are a few examples of guardrails you can set up as a teacher:

- Don't share your personal phone number with families.

- Set office hours with families so they know what days/ times you will respond.

■ Pick one day to stay late at school.

■ Don't add your work email to your phone.

■ Schedule your computer to automatically go to sleep or shut down at a specific time.

■ Set an "out of office" automatic email reply.

■ Set timers/alarms to let you know when you need to leave.

■ Use the "do not disturb" function on your phone.

■ Take your sick days and sprinkle them throughout the year.

Keep in mind that these guardrails are designed to help keep you in the right lane. They do not guarantee a game full of strikes. I once threw a bowling ball so hard it managed to fly over the bumpers and land in the gutter, despite the bowling alley workers assuring me that wasn't a possibility (true story). But, with a little (or in my case, a lot) of extra practice with reinforcing your boundaries, you will find your ball avoiding the gutters more and more often.

YOUR HOMEWORK

Decide on a boundary to put in place. Find what is making you unhappy on a personal level and think about how you can change it. For example, if you're unhappy that you always miss your child's sporting event, put a boundary in place for the absolute latest time you will leave school to ensure you have enough time to make it to the practices and games. This boundary has to become a "nonnegotiable" that you refuse to budge on or let others cross. Write your boundary somewhere visible to you, like on a sticky note around your computer monitor, so it serves as a constant reminder.

Communicate your boundary with the individuals involved. If your boundary is related to parent communication, send an email to families. If your boundary is related to school responsibilities, schedule a meeting with your administration. If your boundary is related to personal time, call or text your family and friends.

Your actions teach people how to treat you, so use this as an opportunity to let go of the guilt and advocate for yourself. State your boundary in a clear and concise way and avoid apologizing or long explanations.

Set up at least three guardrails to maintain your boundary. Ask yourself, "How can I make this easier?" and put those changes into action. Take small steps now that will make it easier to take larger steps later. Write down the three guardrails you want to put in place and cross them off when they're successfully implemented.

Create a list of responses for when your boundary is crossed. It's not a matter of if, but when. People will try to cross your boundary so it's important you are prepared. Here are example responses you can use:

- No.

- Thanks for asking but I'm going to have to pass.

- I appreciate the offer but I'm not taking on new tasks right now.

- I'm honored you considered me but I can't.

- Thanks for thinking of me but I'm not interested.

- No thank you . . . I already have other commitments.

- That doesn't work for me.

- I'm not taking on new things at this time.

■ I don't have the time to dedicate to that right now.

■ I'd love to help but unfortunately can't . . . maybe you could try (insert alternative solution).

Surround yourself with affirmations related to your boundary. There will be moments when sticking to your boundary is uncomfortable, awkward, and challenging. Affirmations can help validate your decision and remind you why you established the boundary in the first place. Write these in a journal, your lesson planner, create a photo album of them on your phone, or save a list in a note taking app on your phone or computer. Here are a few examples you can steal:

■ Boundaries are healthy and necessary.

■ It is not my job to make other people happy.

■ I am allowed to have boundaries.

■ I am worthy of boundaries that prioritize my happiness.

■ I am capable of maintaining boundaries I have set.

■ I deserve to have my boundaries respected.

■ I have a right to express my needs.

In case no one has told you:

You are allowed to make mistakes and ask for help when you need it.

You are allowed to prioritize your personal well-being over your job.

You are allowed to take time off when needed.

You are allowed to say no to extra responsibilities.

You are allowed to take off your teacher hat.

You are allowed to be a person.

More isn't better if it leaves you with less of the good stuff. Teaching has a lot of good stuff, but so does your life outside of the classroom.

The cramp in your side that forms when you laugh too hard

The sparkle of the imaginary lightbulb that illuminates above a student's head when they finally understand a concept

The warm feeling of the sun on your skin when you go for an afternoon walk

The unexpected snow day that both you and your students secretly were hoping for

Find the good stuff and don't let go because the good stuff is what makes all the hardships, challenges, and struggles you experience along the way worth it.

YOUR FINAL ASSIGNMENT

You've been taught the lessons. You've had time to practice the skills. You've done the homework (hopefully). Now it's time to demonstrate your learning with one final assignment: be a first class teacher.

If you've been paying attention, you already know what you need to do to get a passing grade.

- Practice what you teach and have the same expectations for yourself that you have for your students.

- Instead of being a teacher of all trades, become a master of one because you can do anything but you can't do everything.

- Realize relationships aren't built in a day, but they are always worth building.

- Pencil in your plans but be willing to use the eraser because flexibility is key.

- Recognize that what a student throws up must come down, so anticipate the possible messes and be ready to clean them up.

- Remember there is a solution for every problem, so when teaching gives you stress, you can always go out to recess.

- Be ready to add the bells and whistles but remember they don't have to be fancy.

- Stop comparing yourself to other teachers because the classroom isn't always cleaner on the other side.

- Don't get your stickers in a twist because teaching is personal but it doesn't have to be taken personally.

- Realize you can't have your apple and eat it too because every choice comes with a cost.

The realities of teaching may not always align with your expectations. The crystal-clear vision you had for the profession when you first graduated quickly will become distorted and blurry as you transition into your new identity as a teacher and encounter situations you weren't prepared for. Don't worry, this feeling of "I don't know what I'm doing" isn't your fault and it doesn't last forever. Your confidence as a teacher expands day by day as you gain experience, grow through what you go through, and come out stronger on the other side.

When you enter your classroom, whether it's for the first time or the hundredth time, you never know exactly what's waiting for you. Every single day is like turning to an empty page in a book still being written. That uncertainty is intimidating if you focus on all the blank pages ahead. Instead, choose to focus on the beautiful story you are in the process of writing. You get to be the author of your own story as a teacher, so make sure you are writing one worth reading.

ABOUT THE AUTHOR

Michelle Emerson is a former classroom teacher who now supports new and veteran teachers around the world through professional development workshops, videos, and resources. She taught second grade, fourth grade, and served as her school's e-coach, helping teachers integrate educational technology in their instruction for seven years in Maryland before transitioning out of the classroom to develop educational resources and provide professional development to teachers full time. Today, Michelle produces educational videos for teachers on her YouTube channel, Pocketful of Primary, shares productivity tips on her podcast, Teaching to the TOP, and presents workshops at educational conferences and schools across the country. She co-authored *The Edupreneur's Sidehustle Handbook* and has been featured as an educational specialist on the *Today* show twice. She believes all teachers should feel empowered by their career instead of overwhelmed and seeks to help educators master their profession and create a work-life balance through her tips and strategies. Michelle currently resides in Austin, Texas, with her husband, Billy, rambunctious dog, Ember, and two cats, Luna and Zora.

To learn more about Michelle, visit her website at www .pocketfulofprimary.com or follow her on YouTube, Instagram, and Facebook @pocketfulofprimary.

INDEX